PRAISE FOR NICHOLAS MOSLEY

"When unmistakably brilliant writing is combined with natural insight, the result is likely to be most impressive. Nicholas Mosley writes realistically, with an admirable craft and surging talent."

—*New York Times*

"Mosley is ingenious and cunning. . . . Anybody who is serious about the state of English fiction should applaud Nicholas Mosley's audacity—his skill is unquestionable."

—*Spectator*

"Mosley is that rare bird: an English writer whose imagination is genuinely inspired by intellectual conundrums."

—*Guardian*

"Nicholas Mosley is a brilliant novelist who has received nothing like the recognition he deserves—either at home in England or in this country."

—*Saturday Review*

OTHER WORKS BY NICHOLAS MOSLEY

FICTION

Accident

Assassins

Catastrophe Practice

Children of Darkness and Light

Corruption

The Hesperides Tree

Hopeful Monsters

Imago Bird

Impossible Object

Inventing God

Judith

Look at the Dark

Meeting Place

Natalie Natalia

The Rainbearers

Serpent

Spaces of the Dark

NONFICTION

African Switchback

The Assassination of Trotsky

Beyond the Pale

Efforts at Truth

Julian Grenfell

The Life of Raymond Raynes

Rules of the Game

Time at War

The Uses of Slime Mould: Essays of Four Decades

EXPERIENCE & RELIGION
A LAY ESSAY IN THEOLOGY

NICHOLAS
MOSLEY

DALKEY ARCHIVE PRESS
NORMAL · LONDON

Originally published in the United Kingdom by Hodder and Stoughton, 1965
First American edition published by United Church Press, 1967
Copyright © 1965 by Nicholas Mosley

First Dalkey Archive edition, 2006

Library of Congress Cataloging-in-Publication Data:

Mosley, Nicholas, 1923-
    Experience and Religion / Nicholas Mosley. — 1st Dalkey Archive ed.
        p. cm.
    Originally published: United Kingdom : Hodder and Stoughton, 1965.
    ISBN-13: 978-1-56478-424-7 (alk. paper)
    ISBN-10: 1-56478-424-X (alk. paper)
    1. Theology, Doctrinal—Popular works. 2. Experience (Religion) I. Title.
    BT77.M87 2006
    230—dc22

                                                        2006016856

Partially funded by a grant from the Illinois Arts Council, a state agency.

Dalkey Archive Press is a nonprofit organization whose mission is
to promote international cultural understanding and provide
a forum for dialogue for the literary arts.

www.dalkeyarchive.com

Printed on permanent/durable acid-free paper, bound in the United States of
America, and distributed throughout North America and Europe.

To my wife

'We have got to say something to our children'

RELIGION is a mistrusted word now. To the irreligious it doesn't mean anything and the religious are rather ashamed. It referred once to a belief in a power in the world that people had to fit into if life was to be worth living. They thought this was evident from the way the world worked; from man's experience.

It is this that is now out of fashion. Of those interested in the way the world works most are involved in separate scientific disciplines. Many believe in a sort of controlling power but see this as economic materialism or an historical process. Few ask questions about man's active relation to the whole of the world; how he can be in tune with it or even influence it.

To many of course there is no sense in talking like this at all; the world (and such phraseology) is ridiculous.

Even of those who say they still believe in God there are many now who say this not because of their observation or experience but who say God is just knowable through a single revelation—that man must just commit himself (realise he is committed) to this that is imposed. There is even a modern christian idea that God is so unknowable that He might as well not be said to exist;

what man can commit himself to are the sayings and stories of Jesus Christ.

But there are those, probably more than is imagined, who still believe in some power in the world for which there is evidence; which man has to fit himself into, become a certain person for, if he and everything else are to grow and flourish. These people have no common language in which to express this belief; the old ways of expression they have mostly ceased to believe in themselves. But they seem to try to live their lives according to it, even without knowing why.

It is the point of this book to try to say something of religion in terms of what seems to be the way the world works rather than of what might be revealed; not because the latter might be untrue (whatever this means) but because there still has to be some reason for its acceptance. And there is so much known, and felt, now (as always) about the world in areas not covered by materialism, historicism, absurdity, and so on, that it seems odd not to talk about this, especially since these are areas in which men mostly live, and care, and try to organise themselves. They are areas in which theology once talked; but which now seem empty because things there are so difficult to define or prove.

The areas in which things can't be proved but which men mostly care about and live by are to do with their loves, hopes, fears, commitments; their relationships, friendships, marriages, and so on; their children; what they try to fashion and create; what is their freedom and what their helplessness; what is the point of a person, of the world; what is happening and what is its meaning.

To talk about all this, in any form, has always been the business of religion.

I

IT is a platitude nowadays (as always) that the world of convention is breaking up; not only the social structure on which the mechanics of power have for so long rested but the state of mind which made the acceptance of this structure possible: something to do with class, family, morals; but also a sort of tribal mystique which held the whole framework together. The disappearance of this sort of world is seen by many with dismay; we are supposed to be moving towards a social and moral anarchy. This sort of feeling is instinctive: it is backed by statistics about the increase of crime, divorce, delinquency and so on; but these are mostly taken out of a comprehensive context and used as part of an emotional argument. There is little attempt to balance what is obviously anarchic against what might be increasingly orderly; no effort, for instance, to weight an increase in individual crimes of violence against a decrease in violent jingoism in public affairs: or again, no effort to balance an increasing illegitimate birth rate with an increase in the care with which illegitimate babies are treated. There is little such effort because there is nowadays no accepted language in which to talk about these things. What keeps these two sets of observation apart is a difference in characteristics between the people who make them: those who see the world in one way just find it difficult to see it in another. But even amongst sophisticated people a way of thinking which would try to bring such sets of observations together is held to be unscientific and therefore suspect. The contemporary way of making observations is to assess facts in separate categories, in which they remain.

2

Thus the other platitude nowadays which is in direct opposition to the first but is often mentioned in the same sort of context—that the world is far more orderly and intelligent than it has ever been before; that there is less suffering, poverty, ignorance and superstition—this platitude passes the other one by without making much contact with it. The evidence for this second view, those who hold it claim, is simply before one's eyes: there may not be many statistics about it (it is easier to get statistics about violence and destruction than about mercy, tolerance) but to anyone who reads a work of history or imagination of the past it must seem obvious: an eighteenth-century novel or a nineteenth-century social history describe miseries and cruelties which nowadays just do not exist. And together with this view is a feeling that this state of affairs has come about through the increasing ability of man to order his own life; he is supposed to have gained a greater understanding of both his psychology and his surroundings and thus a chance to control them. So the idea that the world is a better place is tied up with the idea that it is man that is making it a better place: and similarly, those who hold the first view, that the world is getting worse, would say that it was man who was making it worse. So that in spite of their opposed directions of view the two sets of opponents in this field seem to have at least this starting-point in common—that man is responsible for his own situation.

3

There is a third and more subtle viewpoint that takes into account these two naïve and opposed attitudes and tries to carry them further. This is done mainly in answer to the second protagonists' claim that there is nowadays less cruelty and intolerance in the world. The answer is — all right, granted that in some superficial sense there is more order and conscience generally, this in fact only makes the forces of evil and chaos all the more powerful when they do emerge; as if these forces had become all the more virulent for having been bottled up. In support of this argument are the obvious examples of recent history —the insane eruption of evil under the Nazis; the existence of enough nuclear weapons to destroy the world. About the Nazis a case has been made out about the very orderliness of the state of mind from which a state of evil flourishes; as if there were a direct correlation between the ability of man to work dedicatedly and efficiently to control his own ends and the vast outbreaks of evil which seem to result. About the Bomb, there is the argument that the very system which has produced the increased order and tolerance—a system of science, education, understanding, and so on—has produced the capacity for destruction. Those who hold this view must find themselves emotionally though unwillingly on the side of those who hold the pessimistically naïve view of paragraph 1: but whereas these are the reactionaries of the satirical imagination—people largely inarticulate except for catchphrases and rhetorical slogans—the people who hold this sophisticated view of chaos and evil are some of the most articulate people today—artists, writers, psychological pundits, and so on. Many of the best works of art being turned out now are a reflection of the world's chaos, even of the possibility of appalling and arbitrary outbreaks of evil. But the point over which the reactionaries and the artists disagree (and which allows them to continue their hostility) is that about man's responsibility. The reactionaries, as well as the progressives, believe that with one more heave man should be able to pull himself over the hill. The artists do not. What modern works of art reflect as well as chaos is helplessness: man can either have a fling against his predicament (existentialists, action painters, jazz musicians, and so on) or he can stoically accept it (anti-novelists, abstract painters, again existentialists, and so on). But whatever he does, he does not alter it.

4

Before asking what might be said in answer to this sophisticated view of chaos and evil, which attempt is the point of this book, it should be seen first why such an answer is desirable (that is, present viewpoints are unsatisfactory) and also possible (that is, there is in fact some sort of accepted answer though at present no words to express it). The unsatisfactoriness of the present common viewpoints is not in their being depressing (even the optimists of paragraph 2 are depressing because naïve) but in the fact that in all of them there is something evaded on their own ground and in their own terms. The reactionaries of paragraph 1 depend on a backward-looking view of some mythical golden age—classicism, ruralism, the faith or rationalism of earlier centuries—they do this to give backing to their belief that man is capable of great and beautiful things: but in fact there is no evidence for a golden age, man has always been a prey to terror, lunacy and destruction (as well as order, kindliness) and it is only in his dreams that he is not; so that what is exposed is not only some fallacy about the past but also the nature of the reactionaries' illusions about the present. There is no evidence, that is, that man (social man) ever gets over the hill. The optimists, when confronted with facts or threats of contemporary evil, frankly turn their backs: they say—'I don't understand about the Nazis and Jews;' 'I don't think anything can happen about the Bomb.' When confronted with the case for evil resulting from the very sort of orderliness they encourage, their reactions are usually angry. And even those who hold to the third view—the sophisticated people of expression—in fact, though as always more elusive, seem to be involved in some contradiction at the heart of their position: for if it is true that the world is chaotic and arbitrary then their position as writers, thinkers, artists, and so on, is impossible—which it is not. For any statement of profound meaning and impressiveness such as they produce in fact invalidates the impression that such a statement is mostly trying to make: however much it suggests that the world is chaotic, that is, its recognisable validity as a work of art (or process or thought) is evidence that the world is different. This is more than the difficulty of saying 'the truth is there is no truth'; it is a paradox of feeling and living too. Very few people do in fact live as if the world were meaningless: people certainly do not create as such. There is a common acceptance even here of something different.

5

This implies the second sort of attempt—to see how a further step in understanding might be possible because there is some common experience of it even if at the moment few words to express it. This common experience is partly simply that there is an enormous amount of joy, energy, order, significance in the world that does not get expressed by artists and thinkers of any subtlety now, and which gets hopelessly vulgarised by those with none. This can be dismissed as self-deception also by anyone who wishes; but it is easier to deceive oneself into misery than into happiness. And there is some hope nowadays even on the deeper and more alarming levels; some hidden expectancy (rather than admit which we would rather die, so unfashionable is it) but which nevertheless most people do live by in spite of the few marvellous prophets of disaster and thousands of cheerleaders who pour out their sad words each day. For in spite of (or rather as well as) our knowledge of chaos, helplessness, there is in fact some growing vision of tolerance now; some seeing of the other person's point of view, some lack of passionate prejudice, some objectivity and some trust. This is of great importance even if negative: with lack of illusion there is an understanding which can grow. We are not so vindictive in justification of our own position any more—or only the most inarticulate are. The articulate seem to be being driven just by knowledge towards more tolerance: it is almost impossible for instance to imagine nowadays a really intelligent and self-conscious anti-semite or anti-negro; impossible to imagine a good fascist work of art. In spite of last-ditch stands it is impossible to believe that in twenty years we will still be hanging people judicially or in fifty will be sending men to prison for homosexuality. There is even this increased tolerance in political events; for instance in England the efforts of nuclear disarmers to disrupt the Government have come to a peculiarly quiet end; as if even those who held such passionate views saw the relativeness of their own position, as if the forces of law and order, in spite of losses of temper, had respect for the integrity and even the function of those against them. All this is very different from the savagery of previous clashes between reactionaries and anarchists. It is true of course that there is an enormous amount of self-deception now which leads to lies and spurious rhetoric (the anti-negro who says that what he does is for the negro's good; the self-delusions and fears of the anti-homosexual) and in a sense this is the real evil of the present age—a fog in which words, and thought, have lost their clear meanings. But this confusion is partly due to what was noticed earlier—the lack of an intelligent language in which to discuss important things. What is required is a way of thinking which will take account of both the hope and hopelessness, responsibility and helplessness, the good not in spite of but together with the evil. And this, at the moment, we have not got.

6

The lack of this sort of language comes partly from the

necessary scientific temper of the time in which things are considered in separate categories and partly from the distrust (perhaps also necessary) that articulate people have for a sort of comprehensive word- and theory-spinning which, God knows, has led to fatuous and dangerous rhetoric in the past. But the lack of such a language among intelligent people means that the field is left open to the self-deceivers and pedlars of slogans: it is all the easier for a South African politician, for instance, to speak convincingly and ridiculously about morals and the purpose of life if few people of intelligence are speaking of these things at all. Once the language in which these things were discussed was religious: but this has fallen into such decay that it is forsaken even by those who might be thought closest to it—even clergymen are denying the usefulness of 'religion'. This revolt against religious language is understandable; it has suffered as much as any from windy rhetoric in the past. But a lively religious language has in fact always been little to do with rhetoric or even argument; it has been an artistic language—religion has been written in poems, parables, stories—and the decay of religion is inevitably connected with the decay of these. For a long time man has tried to argue, even be logical, about religion; perhaps, growing up, he has had to try to do this about everything. But one of the achievements of modern philosophy is to have destroyed the case for a logical language of religion (whatever this might have meant); and it is logical language that has done

19

this. But with the withdrawal of people with artistic talent into solitariness and darkness there has been the death of the proper sort of religious language too—just as perhaps there is a limitation in these kinds of works of art. Art was once to do with significance, meaning, connections; so was religion; now, seldom either. This is not to say that artists need to get religion or religious bodies to take art into otherwise moribund systems; but the sort of language required is something still, though perhaps unrecognisably, artistic and religious. What is necessary is the feeling that there is something vital in all this in experience—that we do experience significance, connection, and so on; the meanings of birth and growth and death—and we want to have some language in which to talk about these things because if we don't we'll lose them or they'll go bad on us. This language will be religious in that it will relate to man's experience; also in that this will be partly of something outside him. It will be artistic in what is recognised. Whatever this is (will be) will seem at moments to be quite new; only afterwards to have been there all the time.

7

The sort of language that occurs, then, will come from what is in experience: and what is here is some knowledge of man's present predicament—of the many-sidedness of this. There is nowadays, for instance, the knowledge that man is on the edge of some great crisis; that this is permanent; that he has the power to control his future suddenly for good but it is this very power that may destroy him. He knows these things all at once; it is for this that a language is required. Because of its very complexity it will not be something argued, reasoned in a straight line as it were; but something of attempts, flashes, allusions — a to-and-fro between a person and whatever he has to do and to discover. What it will be saying will not be part of a comprehensive system but things-on-their-own, parables, paradoxes; the connections between which will have to be held and understood with difficulty, not justified. In the sort of instances mentioned there will have to be some recognition that progress in the world probably only does occur at the cost of disaster or some threat of it; but at the same time everyone has to be working against disaster in order that progress can be made. In the matter of the Bomb (perhaps we have to get used to talking like this; suddenly and with difficulty about it) there will have to be realised, at the same time, first, that the Bomb can destroy us all and there's a chance it will; secondly that the Bomb is probably the only thing that will ensure a decent life on earth since without it we'd be destroying ourselves anyway; thirdly that we must all be working hard to get rid of something so immoral as the Bomb. In the matter of the Nazis and Jews (all this has been said before; has always been said in art, literature; now perhaps has to be made commonplace) what we have to carry is the realisation that this is a history of unique and horrifying wickedness; that without it we should probably not be so much exorcised now and potential victims not rescued; that we must fight passionately against such things happening again; that it is probably only by such things happening that man will move to further tolerance and understanding. All these things are true, difficult, dangerous. We do not like saying them at once because we feel we are making a nonsense — mixing moral imperatives and detached observations. But this is in fact the sort of view that we do have of the world — it is in this light that intelligent men do carry on, even the world seems to carry on, and it is only some failure of nerve that prevents us talking like this and causes confusion. Also this is (as has been said) the language of art — something not single-faced but held between opposites; saying everything at once; a spark between poles. And lastly, where in fact some such language as this does exist (a few odd corners) it does turn out to be a language of hope — of some affirmation of the world again — as if it only needed this effort (the sort of effort that is always needed; to comprehend something that is there and difficult) to produce the spark that is not a choice of either one side or another but a recognition of both; of the world that produces this understanding; which produces an experience of goodness (if that is the word) apart from and beyond the polarity of evil and goodness, if only the attempt is made to comprehend it. Perhaps this is the point. Psychology has taught us that disease is caused by the refusal to admit what is, in a sense, known. This presupposes that if everything were admitted, there would be health. We admit this nowadays about ourselves; religiously this would be about the world.

8

OF the two great modern religious prophets, Freud and Jung, it was Freud, as precursor, who talked of what had to be done to break out of the blindness of the past—of a sort of baptism, as it were, by which a person would enter a state of grace. This process was to do with realising something about unconsciousness and helplessness: admitting the existence of a pervasive instructive drive which conflicted with the demands of both the conscious individual and society, confessing some fear and hatred caused by incidents in the past which were symbolic of the inner confusion and to do with one's parents and almost the whole race. It was taken as scientifically observable that there was this struggle within man; something which if left to itself would cause even more confusion and about which action had to be taken in by a process both self-enquiring and ritualistic—that is, involving one's own efforts and those of another. (Why Freud thought his theories were antithetical to christianity is a mystery only graspable in terms that both Freud and christianity would understand—that connections so disturbing have to be denied.) The process of psychoanalysis is in these ways like an evangelical conversion: there is the recognition of a predicament of disease and feelings of guilt; a turning towards someone or something else to find help; and the eventual experience of the burden being removed, of freedom and strength and light. What was not mentioned so much by Freud was what sort of thing was supposed to happen then: or rather, the question of whether it was true that there was some once-and-for-all conversion (as sometimes seemed to be implied) or was this a process that went on through the whole of life (which in experience it obviously did). There was also the question of what was man's rôle in all this; was he an active agent in conversion, or did it just occur to him?

9

The language Freud used about this process was to do with his description of the mind as composed of id, ego and super-ego. Id was primitive instinctive animality; ego was formed by the restraints imposed on the id by civilisation and society; super-ego was an idealistic and driving conscience which arose from guilt about the past but also (because of its achievements) was the highest mental state of man. It was in terms of the conflict between these three things and the attempt to reconcile them that psychic life was carried on and the success or failure of it could be judged. But there was a confusion here within these definitions. Originally Freud spoke of just the struggle between the outside world and the id and of the necessity for the sake of health for these to be balanced. But what was it that did the balancing? The ego was spoken of sometimes as that which had the power to balance; but it had been described originally as something which just happened to the id—a modification of the id as a result of the pressures of reality— and this passive description seemed essential to the whole Freudian system in which power, or driving-force, came always from the outside or the unconscious. At a later stage the super-ego was brought in to explain observable phenomena about the sense of right and wrong; but it was never the super-ego that did any controlling; rather, in spite of its rôle in making civilisation possible it was a force which in its blindness was much the same as the id. Here again the ego was sometimes spoken of as the controlling factor between the two unconscious forces on either side; but it was described like this only in the context of the practical value of psychoanalysis—what hope there was for a person to be healthy rather than diseased—and in theoretical discussion there was still no mention of what this controlling power might be, by what means its power was manifest. Freud had to have some answer to the question of what it was that did the balancing because if he did not—if nothing was to be made psychically better except by chance—then there was no point in Freud (or any other psychiatrist) carrying on. It was to justify this that the ego (the analyst's, if not the patient's) was sometimes spoken of as that which could choose and decide; but once this context was no longer under discussion—once Freud was writing about the theory of psychoanalysis rather than the use of it—he did not talk like this about the ego or indeed about anything. The ego was once more defined as something to which things occurred rather than that through which someone (or something) did any occurring: and the whole question of free-will, or even the sense of this question, was implicitly denied.

10

What Freud was clear about was that something cathartic had to happen about the past before there could be any light in the present; and in this he was perhaps right not to talk too much about freedom, just as evangelical determinists are probably right, because it does seem mysterious how some people have burdens lifted off them and others don't. And Freud did create a language in which to talk about these things—to talk about guilt, fear, the resistances to admitting these and the possibilities of absolving them, the ways in which we are haunted by our past which we see clearly in others but find so alarming to admit in ourselves. Freud gave us this language quite apart from psychoanalysis—a language to talk of fundamental things which we didn't have before but which, having it now, allows us to do something about them. But the point here is that this language is from the very beginning paradoxical: as soon as anything is said about the id, the unconscious, sexuality, and so on, there is the recognition that this is both the very stuff of life, the all-pervasive creative energy, and also that it has the power of destruction, of overwhelming and stunting the personality. Freud is in fact always talking of these two aspects at once though this is not the style in which he is talking: that is, this is his ambivalent description of the id, the unconscious, and so on, but he does not put it in the form of a paradox —perhaps because he did not admit the force of paradox —a paradox being something of which perhaps the force is seen only if the central (odd) thing is recognised which in some sense has freedom—the power to move between poles. And this is what Freud, and practitioners of other psychological systems, did not see. Again, in the matter of Freud's understanding of parent-child relationship (the chief way in which we are haunted by our past; suffer guilt for something which we have not done and which has even helped us) the language is paradoxical to the point of caricature—children depend on their parents and parents' love and without this there will be grave disorder, yet children hate their parents and have to hate them (even parents have to accept this hate) or else there will also be grave disorder: love and hate have to be spoken of in the same breath. But here again Freud did not seem to speak deliberately in this style; or rather, did not ask what speaking in this style might mean. He saw himself as a scientist; dealing with observation, correlation, classification; not with the significance and possible power of paradoxes. To suggest this—what this sort of language implied; what it was that moved between, held together, the opposites of love and hate—did not seem Freud's rôle.

II

It was left to Jung who did not deny what Freud had said but only claimed he had not said enough, to suggest what might be implied by paradoxes—something about the achieving of a state of freedom and the use of it. Jung did not use the description of the mind as id, ego and super-ego (which had not accounted for the achieving of freedom, of control) but made up a terminology of his own in some ways similar to Freud's but in this vital one different. Jung spoke of the unconscious and the outside world and of the struggle between them; but from the beginning in his description there was some power in consciousness that had its own autonomy; Jung's ego was not something forced upon the id by the pressures of the outside world but something already there, if only an embryo, and waiting to be born into something developed. That part of the personality that was formed as a result of pressures from the outside world was called the *persona*; this was the compromise, the mask, between man and society; and it was as blind as Freud's ego was, but was not Jung's ego, which remained separate from it and in some sense influencing it. On the other side of it were the forces of the unconscious which consisted of those aspects of personality which *persona* left out of account—aspects of thinking, feeling, intuition and sensation which were given inadequate expression by the *persona* and which were thus driven into the unconscious where they took on a life of their own. This power in the unconscious was again in some ways similar to Freud's id; but since by reason of its relation to the *persona* it was given a form over which the ego might have influence, it was again in this vital respect different. The shadow (as Jung called it) was the dark, unadmitted side of a person; describable partly in terms of what aspects of character the *persona* had repressed and partly in terms of just the difference in sexes. For in each of us, Jung said, there is something of the opposite sex; and it is also this that gets repressed. Thus in a man's shadow-side there is something of woman (*anima*) and in a woman's shadow-side something of man (*animus*); and in certain conditions these, together with other unconscious characteristics, attack the ego and even overwhelm it. Nevertheless the rôle of the ego in all this is not helpless: instead of finding itself chivvied by a blind and driving shadow on one side and a blind and driving *persona* on the other (and even surrounded by an implacable and meaningless world) the rôle of the ego is, in Jung's terms, to try to balance what the ego has made of itself (*persona*) and what it has repressed of itself (shadow; *anima*; *animus*) by recognising these things for what they are, by bringing them into consciousness and holding them there. That this is not a straightforward matter, but, again, paradoxical is seen in that what the ego has made of itself and what it has repressed of itself are both, in some sense, justifiable—justifiable because social life (any life) would not otherwise be possible—but also dangerous, because unless they are brought to consciousness they get out of control and virulent. And yet they can never wholly be brought to consciousness; unconscious life renews itself, remains. Jung's language thus allows for conceptions of achievement and control; but also appears, as always, two-faced, containing opposites. It describes demands which are met, but also situations which go on through the whole of life, are not settled.

12

To the question of what exactly it is that does this achieving and controlling—what the ego is, what is its power?—Jung had no more answer than anyone would have to the question of, say, what is electricity? But he did say that this power was observable; said things about how it could be recognised and used, and what happened then. Whereas Freud spoke of the helplessness out of which it was necessary to be rescued by conversion (as it were) Jung spoke of what a person might do to learn, to grow, for health; not particularly by conversion—psychoanalysis being only one of the many things that might be required—other things being more vague and yet more practical. What a person (ego) had to do was to apply himself to recognising the truth about himself and the outside world; recognise something about the *persona* and the *anima/animus*; overcome the resistances to this sort of recognition; take what hints he could both from the unconscious (fantasies, dreams) and from daily life; recognise the indications in daily life; do this both by himself and in relation to others; watch, listen. If he was doing this sort of thing—even if he was making an effort to see this sort of thing—then, Jung said, although in the initial stages he would be making these attempts largely in the dark, as time went on, the feeling of hopelessness would begin to change—not that some end, some state of grace, would suddenly appear—but rather that the means of continuing the process ever further would be changed —there would be found a new centre, a new development out of the ego; a birth, as it were, which could carry the process on but now not so much in the dark, even in hope. This new centre Jung called the Self. In this (religiously) Jung spoke like the parables of the New Testament in which the kingdom of heaven is not something outside a person which has to be moved into but something inside which mysteriously grows — grows, that is, if certain things are being done quite separate from it. This concept of the Self is very important. At first the ego is struggling with the rival demands of the *persona* and the shadow/*anima*/*animus* and the outside world—and probably seeming to fail, because nothing is happening. At this stage there may have to be some help (as in Freudianism) from outside. But then, if this process is persevered with, something at the right moment often occurs—at the moment, perhaps, when the ego seems exhausted—there is some release, take-over, not into a state of peace but into a new form of experience (personality) which although still faced with a continuing process yet sees this with meaning, and courage, even if alarmed. That this sort of thing happens, Jung said, is observable. But the whole validity of the description of this sort of process has depended on a peculiar mode of trust—trust that if one keeps on with these sorts of effort then in fact something will happen as is claimed; trust also, to make sense of this, that there is something apart from oneself working, if one lets it, for what one hopes to be achieved. For the point of this sort of understanding is that something happens apart from (thought permitted by) the will of the person attempting it—while the person's will, though trustfully, is directed to something else. There has to be this faith, that is, in things apart from oneself being

purposive—in something in a person's unconscious working for the person to be whole—requiring, as it were,
the birth of the new Self. And because what a person
has to face are instances in the outside world as well as
in the unconscious, there has to be this sort of faith
about the outside world too. A person has to trust, in
fact, that there is a scheme of things both in the unconscious and in the material world that has within it
what is working towards his own proper functioning and
health.

13

It was this view of the world—not only the inner
world of the mind but also the outer world of event
and history—that brought against Jung a certain hostility.
By it Jung seemed to be claiming some power for magic
—for a dynamic connection between the microcosm of
man and the macrocosm of the world such as had not
been considered seriously since the development of
reason. Jung himself was not very explicit about all
this: like Freud, he wanted his work to be 'scientific';
thinking it of little value if it was not. Thus in his
attempts to justify what might be magic he was let
into the compilation of weird statistics and inconsequent
examples; not realising that there might be some truly
observed evidence about the behaviour of individuals
and instances apart from a scientific method which is

to do with repetitions and statistics. But Jung did face
what he had observed; also used a language that would
face its implications: his efforts to claim that this process
was 'scientific' only obscured what he was trying to say
and did not detract from his observations nor the evidence.
He was always talking about what people did experience
and what they knew they experienced—only found it
difficult to talk about. In this he was truly scientific.
But just as Freud's explanation of phenomena stopped
short of the observed experiences of freedom and control,
so Jung, though seeing these, yet stopped short of suggesting what the total scheme or framework might be
within which (and only within which) such freedom
and control could operate. For there are two factors
necessary for a concept of freedom: the first is the idea
of the thing, the will, at the centre, which is free; and
the second is the idea of the surrounding order, con-
nectedness, within which the free-will or act can operate.
The concept of freedom in a sort of void, a vacuum, is
unimaginable: for a person to experience freedom he has
to have a sort of faith that the world is such that the
free act means, effects something. This is what Jung, in
what he was describing, knew; but he did not, again,
seem to admit it in his style. For it is true that such a
belief entails a trust in something which might be called
magic—in some connection beyond observable cause-
and-effect between what a person is doing and what is
happening; in some such effectiveness between the

person and the larger world. Jung, wanting to be scientific, assembled his statistics about the workings of the psyche; once (in his essay on *Synchronicity*) tried to do the same about the connections between these and the outside world; tried to 'prove' these things—and made them almost unimaginable. For in fact (and this is what he did not admit) the whole business of meaning, significance, a-casual connection (Jung's own phrase) and so on, is outside the realm of science, of controlled and repeated experiment: it is in the realm of the individual, the particular, which still may (or may not) have some autonomy in spite of being part of the predictable and seemingly constant scheme of casual laws. It may be predictable, that is, that out of a million entities (even human beings) certain percentages will do one thing or another; what is not always predictable (and science does not claim it is) is what each of these entities will at any moment do. It is with the recognition of this, and the imaginative (not scientific) grasp of its possible effects—the grasp of such autonomy, on its own, concerning (influencing) some total understanding (occurrence)—that even in this scientific age there is a feeling of freedom and of meaning. This is the area within which and about which art exists; novels and poems are written and pictures sometimes painted. And the truth, the authority, of a work of art, does not depend on something analysable, provable; it is self-evident. This is the area, again, of religion. Jung recognised the therapeutic effects of religion but did not believe in what is usually called religion—except that by his time of course religion was not really religion, though it was something of what Jung himself seemed to be trying to make it. The peculiar position had arisen in which there were recognisably a mass of experiences which might be called religious—experiences of people both in what they truly cared about in themselves (their freedom, power, and so on) and of their understanding of the outside world (again, what to do about it, how to control it); and these were only describable in terms of paradoxes that were religious; but science was always being called in to classify and relate these experiences, or else to say, because they were unique, that they did not exist. Men were (are) in fact always running their lives as if they had freedom; but when they talk about it ignore or deny it.

III

14

THE question of man's free-will is in some sense the most important in life—the question of whether at all, or in what ways, men are able to choose, control things rather than be driven by them—and it is a question over which there is most confusion, both philosophically and ordinarily—perhaps a mark of its importance. We nearly all do live as if we have free-will; yet when we think it seems to be an illusion, we are content to leave it a mystery. This was a question, again, once covered by religion; the whole scheme of religious stories, statements, parables, revolved around what man was supposed to do with his life, what he was able to do, what was his illusion and what in fact his freedom. The decay of religious language has meant that here again there is separation between theory and experience; we do not now talk about how in fact we do behave. And this has happened at a time when what little religious understanding is left is emphasising that man now has to deal consciously with such questions; that he is on his own as it were with his understanding and choices; no longer part of a mystique or group in which such questions were once perhaps not conscious, but understood instinctively.

The question of what man's freedom is—of what can be done between different possibilities—is connected with the question of what ought to be done, because there is no sense in can except in relation to ought—the impression that one thing might be better than another. And what a person ought to, can do, is connected with what might be suggested to him to do; because there is no sense in talking about can or ought except in terms of how a person in practice might be encouraged. Anyone can spin any theory, that is, about possibilities and morals; but these can only make sense if they relate to events; to things that people might say in situations. In large-scale affairs it is assumed that man has freedom in the present but it is known how little he has when looking to the past; yet the question is seldom asked—in what ways does what we know of the past and feel in the present affect, together, our understanding of freedom? In small-scale affairs—personal lives such as are written about in novels, plays, and so on—such a question is asked but nowadays nearly always answered negatively; freedom is illusory, man is just an item (though the writer himself does not seem such) in a machine. In psychology there is a language which comprehends these different impressions but which seems reluctant to talk about 'ought' or 'can' directly; which rather directs itself towards something else, a theory, treatment, leaving the understanding of freedom somehow to grow on its own; as if there were no point in talking of this even though it might exist; as if to do so would invalidate its chance of growth. And people nowadays who too easily assume that man has freedom, who talk about it and exhort man rigorously to exercise freedom, these people—the cheerleaders—are received, fortunately, with an almost total mistrust. Thus nothing much is noticed of this sort of thing at all; but this— both the failure of serious people to tell others what they can (ought to) do and that of moralists to have any effect—this is not a failure of courage on the one hand and of receptivity on the other; or rather, it need not be; it is more like a recognition that there is in fact no easy way of talking about this, however much it is vital. The difficulty in this talk is not just a matter of being able to make only particular observations and not general ones; this is still a modern moralist's way out, enabling him to go on exhorting individuals though he cannot theorise—though he is received with the same mistrust and incomprehension. Rather what has come to be realised nowadays (and it is this that is the opposite of loss of nerve or sensitivity) is that it is the point of this sort of question that it cannot be approached directly; that when we want to talk about man's freedom —about what man can and ought to do—we cannot talk directly about such-and-such an action or another in the outside world; we have to talk, rather, about what will make the person concerned with the sort of person he is required to be; required, that is, for whatever action will afterwards occur. We can talk, perhaps, about the sort of things that he can (ought to) do to become this sort of person: but it is no good talking about much else, and afterwards talk may be unnecessary. That is, in all talk of freedom, morals, and so on, what is worth talking about is not what a person ought to or can do but the sort of person he might or could be. There may be certain actions to be recommended about this, but these will not be to do with the things originally under discussion: these (and whatever is done about them) are of less importance.

16

For instance (we do not often talk about mundane instances because there is something ludicrous about them) when, in everyday life—in a matter, say, of whether or not to give in to one's wife or husband in an argument; whether to be firm or tolerant with a child—in a situation when a person has the impression of his ability to choose, of freedom, what such a person experiences at these moments (he will only be conscious of freedom if the case for one choice is not obvious; if it is, he will be compelled) is a condition in which argument about the choices themselves (argument either within himself or with another) does not much matter.

A case can usually be made out for each of several actions; the very fact that a person seems to be experiencing freedom means he is outside this sort of persuasion. At these moments (which grow more frequent the more one recognises complexities; the less one is simply compelled) it seems to be realised that the question of what directly has to be done is in the first place irrelevant; what matters is the state of mind, true motives (or lack of motives) of the person doing it. If these are right then the action (whatever it is) will be right; the rightness will be that which is transmitted by the state of mind, the personality. There is something of this not only in experience but in law, in moral philosophy. What makes a course of action right is only in some later way dependent on its effects; in the first place upon a state of mind of the person doing it—which should take into account possible effects. But if these latter are known beforehand—if their quality of good or evil is admitted— then there is no moral problem: people do not in fact do actions which they know and admit are evil—if they have some conception, that is, of evil (some have not)—unless they claim they are doing a lesser evil in the face of a greater, when the question is begged anyway. But in considering any course of action in the future (a moral predicament) what is discussed (thought about) has to be the state of the personality: an argument about possible effects, though part of the discussion, is at the mercy of rationalisations and self-deceptions and it is only by facing these (the personality) that rightness will be encouraged or ensured. This is not to deny the objectivity of evil (that there are things good and evil) but a recognition of what can, and cannot, be done about it. The world is littered with the results of people aiming at good and achieving evil; working out what they think will be good effects, that is, and finding them evil; and it cannot be pretended that such choices, as opposed to results, are unambiguous. In order to achieve some confidence about how to do good a person has to be the sort of person who chooses good without knowing how he does it—not just by instinct, as in the past, but perhaps by trusting his knowledge of what makes him such a person. And there is some further trust here—trust that if intentions are in fact good then there will be good results; and if evil results from them then what has been shown is that the intentions were not good. Without some trust such as this there could be no morality; which, in spite of everything, there is. But both these sorts of trust—trust that there is some means of being this sort of person, and trust that if one is then what follows will be good—both these are religious trusts; only comprehensible religiously.

17

What is being noticed here is something about the way in which people do behave: people do face themselves (or others) at certain times with questions about what to do, what it is possible to do; and these are at important moments of their lives, not at dream-like edges where they have been driven by extremity but at the centre where they face what is always their responsibility—their possibilities of growth and change. In the sort of example that has been mentioned—a quarrel between a husband and a wife; whether or not to give in or what to do about it—there is at first the experience of helplessness; this is how such situations are usually written and talked about, under compulsion, even violently; and the helplessness remains so long as it is imagined that the area of freedom is within the argument—within the business of persuading the other person that one thing is right and another wrong. But what has been learned nowadays (what we have been told by the modern religious prophets) is that the area of freedom is not here at all; it is in oneself, in the possibilities of understanding and changing oneself, not in the hope of changing another person, or not directly, at least. The husband/wife quarrel is a predicament in which freedom is longed for and almost always lost; but if attention is directed not to the argument but inwards to oneself—to one's own motives, honesty, intentions (what Jung would call the *anima/animus*; the shadow)—then in fact one is no longer compelled; one has freedom, here, to persuade, change or at least to recognise (which has the same result) something of oneself; to change one's anger, weakness, which is wrong, even if in the thing at stake (though this is irrelevant) one may be right; the point of naming (recognising) the shadow being that it can thus be changed (and this only be changed) and thus mysteriously change the rest. For this is the point: first, that one part of oneself can change (allow to change) another part; the consciousness, if it has the courage, has the freedom to change the unconscious: and secondly, that by doing so, it is not only this that is changed but there comes about the change of the things outside that could not be changed otherwise. Thus in the matter of the husband/wife quarrel, a person, by recognising his own compulsion—by exercising his freedom, his only freedom, to recognise and exorcise this compulsion—can alter the quarrel, end it; in fact alter the other person. He can do this no other way: it is the best he can do.

18

Another example—If there is a question about whether or not to do some act of violence—to take up arms, for instance, to fight (a predicament of the large-scale world)—what a person will properly consider, what will govern the rightness of his choice (again unless an answer is obvious which it is not) will not be in the first place a matter of theories or practicalities but rather of what kind of person he is, his state of mind, honesty. One man in certain circumstances might properly do violence; another in the same might not. All this is known, admitted—we are tolerant nowadays about people of different kinds and convictions—we only have not got the language for it. (As is seen in discussions about the Bomb; people of blatantly good intentions cannot communicate). If two people are found in such an argument—one recommending force and the other against it—what will make their argument profitable is not the business of debate (except in a negative way; the function of debate being that energy shall be exorcised, passions exhausted by talk) but rather the matter of the honesty with which each person considers his own motives and authority—this authority depending, as before, not on a man's ability to make out a reasoned case to compel others, but on his courage in facing what might be his rationalisations and self-deceptions in himself; his freedom not to be taken over and blinded. There is a necessity in all this that people shall know facts—know what they are talking about and the probable results of what they are talking about—because without such knowledge freedom, again, cannot operate; cannot act in a void. Moreover there is even some trust that knowledge itself will help to a right decision; that there is something in facts working to a right decision; but not on their own, because facts can be (often are) used by blindness and compulsion. In an argument, then, what will be profitable for another

person as well as oneself (or rather, what will allow
another person or oneself together or differently to do
what is right) is just this authority through honesty —
honesty in the face of facts and probabilities and not
at the mercy of what is imagined from them — honesty
about oneself and even, if asked, about what seem the
self-deceptions of another person. Authority is a matter
of what one is rather than of what is done and said:
and there is nothing better that can be achieved than
this, even in the face of evil. Some will use violence
and some will not: the effect will depend on what is done
freely; even morally.

19

There remains the question of what this authority is;
how to achieve it; what more to say about it other than
platitudes about trying, listening and learning about
oneself and the world, turning one's back on nothing
however bizarre and alarming. Again, this was once the
business of religion: religion was what let men be free,
gave men an area of freedom; suggested what to make
of themselves in it. Religion was about the sort of
disciplines, guides, there were in the achieving of this
in oneself; about what could be done about it for others.
Religion was not morality: morality was a means of
becoming free, but religion was the business of making
morality seem irrelevant. Religion gave (and talked

47

about) the possibility of this and the faith in it—faith, that is, that if certain efforts were made then certain experiences would result; that even if there were little efforts but still faith then something could still result (had in fact resulted). Religion did not compel, did not threaten: it described what was offered to a person, which was freedom; and even if this was not accepted, freedom was still there. It was the language, the stuff of life, by which men learned to be not machines; that in fact they were not. In all this discussion, then, a point has been reached where it has been claimed that religious language is, firstly, the only adequate language in which to talk of anything serious at all (the world and oneself); secondly, the only means of knowing and altering (always necessary) oneself and others; thirdly, the only way of explaining how we ordinarily do act, the faith we do have (though unadmitted) in changing and effecting things. In this view of the world—of an order that is not logical, all-of-a-piece, in which everyone is supposed to be able to persuade everyone else to the same mind, but rather diverse, living, depending on each person being true to his discovery and knowledge—this sort of view is dependent on trust; trust in oneself and in the world; in their relation. This is sometimes supposed to be subjective, anarchic; but is not. What is anarchic is the straining to persuade, to compel: there is enough evidence for this in history. The world is such that its only true objectivity is in such trust;

in the search for and belief in such authority. As has been said—we know all this: it is what we live by; our lives have no meaning except in terms of it. We only don't know how to talk about it. We have grown despairing of the old language of religion: or perhaps never understood it.

IV

20

THE religion of the western world has been christianity; which helped to form that world and which the world now mostly denies. This is due partly to a lack of feeling of need for religion but also to a contradiction in what is seen of christianity. The latter has contributed to the former: people stop caring about what seems to make no sense.

21

Christianity from the outside is seen through an institution, the church, and a book, the bible. Orthodox christianity has understood an interdependence between these two: the institution got the book and the book justifies the institution: the authority of the one depends on the authority of the other. But what the outside world sees is not polarity but contradiction. What is understood from the book seems to have nothing to do with the institution.

The book, the bible, is a collection of stories, histories, poems, sayings, and so on. It is obviously not an argument; not a work of explanation. Its authority, like that of a work of art, depends on something intrinsic; or rather (the same thing) upon the response of a reader. That it should have this sort of authority—that of a work of art rather than that of argument, explanation—is in keeping with what has been said earlier; that it is the function of art to show meanings, significance, in a way that argument can never do. The bible talks about the meaning of life on earth; what man is here for, what he is to do. In talking of this a work of art (the bible) just puts something (itself) before the reader and leaves him to make what he likes of it. One of the things talked about is freedom; the point is not to persuade, compel.

23

But this understanding of the bible, however obvious, has been difficult for the institution, the church, to accept. An institution, except in the first instances, does not want stories, poems. These are there to give it impetus; only art is creatively contagious. But after this an institution wants to perpetuate itself. Although its business has been, and is, the perpetuating of freedom (the putting of itself before others to enable them to do what they like with it) it finds that it is recommending itself; persuading others to accept itself.

24

The institution depended too much upon the book ever consciously to deny it: but what the institution could do (did) was to suppose that the book was something else—not a work of art, poems, stories; but rather a collection of facts and recommendations. Sometimes it made out that the bible was something called literal truth (whatever that might mean); sometimes something called moral truth: in either case to do with definitions, regulations, and the necessity of keeping them. Many people still think of the bible like this: they are helped by the church's way of reading it cut up and mixed in bits and pieces, which renders the whole thing unintelligible.

25

If the bible is read straight through it appears that there are in fact two or three chapters to do with rules and regulations and of these no christian pays any attention whatsoever. They are to do with things like hygiene, and cooking. Also the largest part of the bible—the Old Testament—is specifically about man's attempt to live by rules and regulations—his impression that he was supposed to do this—and his failure. The whole sequence of stories, histories, poems, and so on, has an overall pattern—in the way that all works of art have a pattern; not spelt out, again, in argument or explanation but just there for anyone to see it—and this pattern is, in the Old Testament, the story of man's understanding that he was supposed to live by rules, that these rules had been imposed by God, and that all he had to do was obey them. There were supposed to have been certain arrangements between God and man (that Adam should not eat of the tree; the Israelites should obey certain commandments) which, if man honoured, then God would keep his part of the bargain and see that man prospered. If not, then man would not. But the whole moral of the story was that man never could (never did) keep his part—however much he felt he should have done. Adam did eat the tree; the Israelites did not obey the commandments: so that man seemed not only incapable of doing what was demanded of him but seemed perpetually being punished for this. This not only made man's position miserable but also seemed to suggest something absurd about God. God, in this sort of understanding, did little else except punish. But it was God who had made man; he thus appeared eventually as something monstrous—more monstrous than man. Towards the end of the Old Testament, among the minor prophets, the air is one of almost total futility and gloom. It is as if it is beginning to be recognised that if this concept of God and of what God wanted was true, then not only was man's predicament horrible but there was something about God not worth believing in.

26

(What is being spoken of here is man's understanding of God; not God himself. God (whatever this might be) is unknowable in words; what is knowable (or might be) is men's experience of God. It was men who wrote the bible: the bible is, in an obvious sense, the story of man's understanding of God—not of whatever might be God's understanding of himself. The authority of the bible (self-evident like that of a work of art) is authority in the matter of its being true about man's understanding; not about God, knowable as himself. It is true that the very possibility of using, and understanding the meaning of, words like 'true' and 'authority' suggests the existence of something which might be called God: but this is still only saying that we have these experiences. Once man imagines he can talk about God directly, he finds himself defining and ordering God about; telling God what He is and what He is to do.)

The New Testament starts in quite a different style. After the frightful gloom of the end of the Old, in which the only people who seemed to make sense were raving, there is suddenly stillness, order, light. Something quite different is happening. There is someone, some people, talking not in the shadow of despair (the knowledge that man is supposed to live by rules but can't) nor unbelievableness (the feeling that God only punishes) but in some certainty that everything, however odd, is all right. Even the rules, still there, may be all right. They may both matter and not matter; there is something else. This is felt both in the style and in what is said. It is an experience that happens to a reader when he reads the book right through. It is like conversion.

28

What this new understanding is is not a denial of rules but something apart from them; not a contradiction now (the despair that rules are imposed and impossible) but even a recognition of them in hope; making the impossibility not matter, even possible. The rules were to do with men's understanding of the way things worked, ought to work; a true experience but unattainable. What is new is something about men's trust, spontaneity; man finding things out for himself how things can also work, what is possible; the opposite of rules, but perhaps possible as a result of them. The language here is immediately paradoxical: the clearness, stillness, of the New Testament depends on its being paradoxical. On the one hand there is everything from the Old—the demands, the knowledge, the impossibilities (the knowledge that life is like this—that we are called on to do things that we can't)—and on the other this quite new liberation, gained partly by honouring the rules but also fighting them; tied to and at the same time free of them. The point, all the time, is that this liberation is not into some opposite order from that which went before; not away from the law into anything equally simple, single-faced; but deliberately into something difficult, two-faced; into the world of poles, polarities (both spontaneity and law) within which there is freedom to move. The new half of this polarity (opposed to, but contained together with law) is to do with acting freely, acting for others, acting for oneself (the same thing); in the trust both that it is possible to do this and, if it is done, that what happens will be all right. It is a doing of things instinctively in response to the moment; doing what people ask of one, asking things for oneself; not taking thought about reasons but acting from the heart, which has been discovered by this liberation. Evil in this sort of attitude is the deceiving of oneself; not being true, not facing facts; being in-

56

capacitated by fear. But there is a paradox even around this spontaneity because this on its own too is as impossible as the old laws were: men cannot help deceiving themselves, cannot do what they are asked for, or want, instinctively. But still between the two impossibilities there is the third thing that is possible—the freedom—something which can choose, move (be chosen) just because there are these extremes to move between. There is a choice, that is, within the area between law, the recognition of the way things work (ought to work), and spontaneity, the altering (or creation) of the way things can work; and it is between these that man is free, and does what he is supposed to do. This is perhaps the only area he has freedom: at either extreme he is to some extent taken over by necessity. (He is taken over even by spontaneity; by freedom.) But his own freedom is in being conscious of, and holding to, his knowledge of (between) the two extremes. What enables him to do this is not itself an action but the ground for action—a sort of courage, or what has been called faith. Faith is that this sort of thing is possible; also that, if a man has it, then the world in some way works for him. These aspects are complementary: there is no faith except that this is what the world is like (that there is some order which corresponds to man's hope); and there is no knowledge of this order, meaning, unless the attempt at faith is made. The world in fact does not seem to have meaning unless there is freedom; man's freedom depends on the world's working for him. These faiths are the same; at first in the dark.

There are obvious parallels here with the language of psychology. Sometimes the experience of christians is like that of Freudians; they are helpless between forces which they only begin to understand and do not control. Faith has to be faith in some break with this past; which comes about by fate, chance, still outside man's doing. And still, after the break, there is some helplessness; the break has been made from one extreme to the other and the person, even though elect, is still driven. But sometimes the experience of christians is like that of Jungians; at the beginning there is darkness but still something that can be done; just something recognised, faced, of what is happening; something recognised in oneself that can do this, even if this is all that can be done. But even in the darkness there is knowledge that it need not always be like this—not faith in just a break but that something will grow from it within which there will be freedom. And if this knowledge is carried, held, then in fact something does grow: there happens, out of sight, what one has had faith in; not just an exorcising of the past but the experience of freedom (Spirit). This takes over; not as a compulsion, an extreme, but as what the person really is. This is the point. This

Spirit is not describable except as that by which the person both does and does not have freedom: that to which he freely gives himself and which then carries him. He both has the choice; is chosen. The language becomes unmanageable.

30

(In talking of the New Testament so much has been quoted out of context to make out a case for anything under the sun—to prove whatever anybody wants to prove under the sun—that it seems improper now to quote: to use quotations to make points the opposite points to which could be made just as glibly. It is this way of using art as a repository of magical slogans that has done the mischief; by it men have been able to pick whatever bits of magic suited them and claim that these were God's: and armed with these, their own projections, to try to impose themselves on others. In suggesting what the New Testament is talking about—the whole of it, not just bits and pieces—it seems better to try to do what the New Testament does; to make statements and leave them, not justify.)

31

The sort of polarity that is being described—that of rules on the one hand and spontaneity on the other and whatever it is that goes between—has its paradoxes within its own terms, which is what makes it difficult and sometimes objectionable. The rules in one sense are that which have been found to give framework, reference, order; that without which there can be no freedom because there could be nothing to be free within or free from, there would be no movement in a vacuum. But in another sense they are that which brings petrifaction and death. In christian terms it is the church, the institution, that perpetuates (is the manifestation of) the rules—both as life-giver and destroyer. In a sense the church is opposed to everything that a free man stands for: it is that which Christ fought and which fought Christ: the denier of truth, the torturer of the honest, the servant of mammon. All this is too much felt now to go on about it: the concern of the church for power, respectability, vanity, money—its obsession with sexual morality and disregard for any other —all this, it is obvious to everyone except christians, is just what stops other people being christians and will go on doing so. But still, opposed to this, there is preserved in the framework of the church (how else could it be preserved?) the truth of the story, the history, the art, the secret. The church is that within which the possibilities of freedom are held; through which is transmitted, beautifully, this experience. (How else could it be preserved except in something so paradoxical?) Within the rigid and self-seeking church have been the things that have given the chance to alter everyone.

Spontaneity, the other extreme, has its own paradoxes; the tragedies of which are also obvious. Spontaneity
is giving, healing, being given to, life. It is also pain,
impossibility, only finding itself in death. People who
live for the moment find something that the rule-keepers
never know—liberation, joy, in a sense themselves. They
also find a running down, a will to extinction, in which
nothing becomes real except themselves—and finally the
vacuum. It is both these sorts of experience that alarm
the conformists; they are experiences of people both
inside and outside christianity, which novels, art, are
written about—that people who commit themselves
simply to their own feelings and their own consciences
are involved in creation but also death. These people are
sometimes reformers who give a huge new impetus to
the world in pain and bloodshed; who sometimes give
pain and bloodshed for a dream. All artists know this
—the closeness of love to death. People who love know it.
Christians, of course, know it centrally. But here it is
different. For this love was given (done) not only spon-
taneously: at least part according to the rules.

In all this, then, whatever happens, is done, is of importance not in so far as it is either obedient or spontaneous but in so far as it is both—as it is recognised as both. It is in this area, again, that there is choice; the existence of right and wrong. The right, here, is the recognition of the freedom to choose; not necessarily in the thing being chosen. The rightness is in the recognition and the holding to it, and the thing is done of itself. And the wrong, here, is the refusal to recognise this polarity, freedom; it is the obsession, in self-justification, with the thing itself. At either extreme the right does not exist because there is no choice but only compulsion: it only exists with both, where freedom happens. Thus in the matter of Christ's death this action was free, obedient, chosen, determined (wanted and not wanted): nothing less describes it. In the matter of the institution, the church, this is only being true when it sees itself both as the guardian of freedom and also the betrayer —the perpetrator of death as well as the life-carrier. The spontaneous man of conscience is being true when he sees himself with the power of gods but at the same time alone, helpless. The whole business of free action, choice, takes place on a level below (above) that of willing what is to happen; rather on a level of holding some complex knowledge and faith in the heart—and then things happening for one. This is the comprehension of opposites—something hardly seen, felt with difficulty, often overwhelmed. That it is there and operative is the matter of faith; its holding is courage. When it is looked at it is not there: what are discernible are its effects.

V

34

RELIGIOUS (christian) language described this sort of experience—listening, learning, acting, in order that something may take over; and the world, the way it works, letting this happen. Religious language once used stories, images, because otherwise the paradoxes became too diffuse. The power of stories and images has lessened, but there is still the experience. Only to talk (write) of it is difficult.

35

What prevents a new use of religious language is, partly, a refusal to see what was the decay of the old. There was a misunderstanding about language; what language does. It is now recognised (except perhaps by the religious) that statements about belief, what is true, are statements about a person's commitment—not statements about an ultimate reality, whatever that may mean. A statement about the nature of God, as has been said, is not a statement about the nature of God (how could it be?) but about our understanding of the way things happen; and the validity of this, in turn, is

shown not just by what we say (we can say anything)
but by the correlation between what we say what we are
and what we do. We can say what we like about the
nature of God—and people may or may not believe us
(we may not believe ourselves). But there is no sense in
not believing what we are and what we do. This is what
we are known by.

36

This sort of thing is accepted by philosophers. There
is no longer an argument about what is understood to
be an object. The philosophers say—for practical purposes we take what seems to be an object to be an object;
but what can be argued about are practical purposes.
Similarly in religious language it is beginning to be felt
that there should be no argument about the nature and
history of God—that such-and-such (in terms of art)
can be taken to be the nature and history of God—
but what we can argue about is man—what he is and what
he is here for. It is this there is evidence (experience)
about. This is not to say there is no such thing as God.
There is an idea, rather, that this is the way to talk about
God.

37

This is more than a change of fashion. At the back of

it is a feeling that to discuss the reality of God is in fact a huge mechanism to obscure man from reality — to make him always be asking questions which have no hope of an answer so that he need not face those which have. This feeling is also to do with what seems to be man's choice to remain within the safety of rules which are not possible for him to observe (the safety of inevitable failure) in order to escape from the freedom which is possible for him but difficult. Thus dogma and theology are felt, now, often to be methods of evading responsibility — man's method of getting out of enquiring what he is supposed to do by wrangling endlessly about what God is supposed to be — which by definition is unknowable. The force of this sort of understanding is only seen if there is some realisation at the beginning of the absurdity of man's defining God (and claiming to know what God wants, orders) apart from man's experience of the world — and of the actual effects of doing this. For centuries, though saying they believed in the unknowableness of God, men have in practice defined him and his wishes so closely that they have killed and tortured for them — and all in the name of love. They have projected, that is, their own compulsions on to God, in order to have an excuse for them. (What other explanation is there?) Thus there is not only the absurdity of this kind of presumption but also its results — the cruelty, hatred, bigotry. And at the back of this, still, is the misunderstanding about language.

The person who is faced with religion is faced at a first stage with some demands upon him—demands that he should be, do, change into something. At this stage there is some falling in love with God (with the idea, experience of God) and in this sense there is the conviction that what is called God is personal and objective —the person being in love with it. There is some projection of the person's experiences (hope; delight; sin) on to another in order to recognise them and make them bearable; also for something to be done about them. Without this there can be no break with the past and no liberation. At this stage, with religious language, there is the feeling of the religious stories (images) being in reality true (which they may be)—and this is not an illusion, but experience; its trueness is in its effects. (This is what is meant by objectivity, the reason why there is meaning in talking about God: the concept of God works; exists because things work.) But still it is an experience that is like love; not an intellectual knowledge but a passionate committal. The intellectual questioning of such a situation (about in what sense such an experience might or might not be 'true') is in one sense unanswerable and in another sense a matter of observing and analysing what occurs. The reason why religious stories might be true (probably are) is not only in the fact but in the type (meaning) of their effects—as opposed to the effects of those who distort or ignore them.

It is only after this stage, when the original love has turned into something different (which it usually does but not always) that there is the danger of this passionate commitment to objectivity being misunderstood—something which was a passion, and a passion that worked, being codified in anxiety and into the illusion of safety. Psychoanalysts talk of the early stage of this sort of process as transference; and then of the necessity of breaking a transference or else it will go bad. Without this break a person starts to use what was once life-giving and necessary (the projection on to another; this being true for a person) as a means for avoiding his own responsibility—the demands of change, of growing up. This coming to terms with one's situation oneself is a hard process; often not achieved, causing damage. In religious terms this danger of not breaking with a too great dependence on objectivity is seen in what actually happens when the original impetus of love dies: then, what was once seen and worked in love (the passionate belief in the story; the freedom and love that the story was about) becomes the codification into rules and the fear of breaking them—perhaps necessary for order, but not to be committed to as the original love once was. For with this codification (different from love) but still held passionately, come the evils of contradiction, a split in the personality (fear and love) a turning of one's back on wholeness, truth. And it is observable in religious history that when this break from projected love, the giving of one's personality to another, is not made when it should be, then in fact what was once love does not linger as a ghost but becomes destructive. There grow various obsessions—the seven devils in the place of the one. This is what is observable in the church: that christians, having ceased to be in love with their beliefs, often not only formalise them into what they are obviously not but thereafter begin to murder and detest one another.

40

It should not be too difficult for christians to understand all this; it is what the story to which they commit themselves is about. The story of the Old Testament is about the impossibility of rules: the Gospels are about man's new understanding of God (God's revelation of himself) as that which man can love (because God loves) and on to which man can transfer his impossibilities and failures (not pretend they are something different) and then God (the experience of God) bearing them, so that man can become free. Then, at the end of the Gospels, there is the story of man having done this (this having been done by God) being required to take on his own responsibility: God is no longer to be seen as something outside a person upon whom (upon the belief in whom) he can project his loves and impossibilities; but something within a person, some spirit (Holy Spirit) by which the freedom that has thus been won can now operate. There is the demand, just, for men to recognise this gift of Spirit: which within them (within the world) will dissolve impossibilities, take over the personality and alter everything. There is also the church which will be the guardian of this Spirit: but in coming to terms with the destructive powers in the world (which also exist; they are not eliminated; only able, if men wish, to be defeated) this guardianship of the church will in a sense be always perverting the Spirit: because of the corruption (polarity) of the world, it will be making out it is something different.

41

It is one of the ironies of religion that all this is spelt out for christians in what they believe yet they do not believe it. The belief, of course, is difficult: if a person begins to understand this that the bible is saying he moves out of a safe world of rules and literalness into something unknown and therefore frightening; in which he is apt to get lost as well as (as the bible says) saved. For instance, it is seen that what has to be done by christians for those who have no feeling for religion is not to do with preaching at them or even simply instructing them (this may be ignored or turned into what it is not) but to do with giving them the chance of falling in love—loving other people, things, themselves, the world. But in order to do this religious people (who are supposed to know about love) themselves have to be lovable—their ability to transmit love depending on their lovableness, and this depending as has been said not on what they say but on what they are. There is in fact some acknowledgement now that it is the rôle of christians not to preach but simply to act in the world, to be. This is what works: nothing happens religiously except through a falling-in-love; which only happens when there are people who are carriers of love, when what is seen through them is the meaning and marvel of the world. But then, this having happened, people are still on their own.

42

Also, it is seen that the attitude towards those who are still truly in love with literalness, the stories, has not to be one of argument either: rather one of realising that this situation (the being in love) is one which is real; is true and fortunate; its language necessary. Without this existence of impetus, objectivity, there probably cannot be change nor agency of change; these are the carriers of love, and others perhaps may not catch it except through such a passionate committal. Thus the stories about God's incarnation, resurrection, and so on, are just there; they are believed in, felt, known, have results. What they mean is difficult; their truth is in their results. Historical truth will seem certain to some and of less importance to others: this does not matter (except to historians: but they, as they go closer towards historical events, find the objectivity in representing them obscure; again more a matter of personal commitment). The central stories of the christian faith can be taken as objectively or subjectively as anyone wishes; there should be no quarrel here that is not due to a misunderstanding about religion and religious language. In any christian there is some commitment to objectivity; all feel, at some time, love, the passionate committal; they know this, if not understand it. Also, in everyone, there is doubt—to be admitted. The point at issue here, and what does matter, is whether whatever is felt is felt truly—and the test of this, again as always, is not what people say but the conjunction of this with what they are and what they do. It is not the people who feel and act truly according to their love and literalness that are the persuaders, destroyers, the christian bigots: it is only those who talk about love but for whom love has died and has been perverted into their own compulsions who deceive themselves and thus are a prey to devils. Similarly it is not those who feel the subtlety, complexity of human experience and language who despise those who are in love religiously; only those who create their own empty dogmas. It may be felt that this sort of understanding—the understanding that what matters is something being felt and acted truly rather than questions of what it is or is not that is true —is a denial of one thing being better than another; even a denial of the appalling power of evil. But in experience in the face of evil (though it is difficult to say this) there is the impression that evil is let in by some madness, some split, some appalling disassociation within people; rather than, however great its power, by some force in the face of which men are helpless. The only way to talk about evil is in terms of what to do about it: and these terms are, finally, those of men trying to do something about themselves—their own honesty in what is their own freedom. This is difficult to say because of the pain of evil and of man's responsibility for it. But at the back of this is the experience that this is the way the world works—that in spite of the power of evil there is a meaning in the world (if such an understanding is observed) which does not destroy evil but in some ultimate sense makes it not matter: that man can defeat evil by being something in himself; that this meaning is to do with the way things change, grow, go through stages—even with pain. It is a function of everyone to have respect for these stages (objectivity, responsibility): there is meaninglessness (even though there is often pain) only when this growth is denied—when it is thought that everything should be in stultification for ever, thus letting in evil and causing destruction.

43

It is for those who have some understanding of all this—who, having loved, try to live (feel) the possibility of freedom (spirit)—that there is needed a new sort of language. What matters is still not primarily what is said but what is done and is: but it is in words that understanding is carried and grows. It has to be understood that this freedom, growth, can happen (perhaps nowadays most frequently) right outside the area of what is thought to be religion and religious language—anywhere where people can learn, keep their ears open and be human. There is in fact this feeling amongst christians now that God (the experience of God) perhaps operates more through what are called the irreligious than the religious. But also there has to be understood the falling in love, the objective language of commitment; that this is one half of the thing that has to be held both at once; that there is the need for everyone perhaps sometimes to go back to the beginning to feel what love is, to find again the seeds of passionate hope and energy. But more than this a religious understanding, new language, will have to talk not only of the need to recognise the roots together with the meaning, but of the day-to-day things a person can do to hold all this; what it means in practice for a man to turn himself (be turned) away from compulsions towards the choice between rightness and nothing. And here, in the first place, there is not much new to be said: it is in the New Testament; no one has done better, and it is there for anyone who wishes. The New Testament is about the kind of thing that has to be done, in freedom, for a person's resurrection and that of the world. But all this (parables, histories, stories, poems) is talking in the face of what might be the imminent end of the world—or at least a person's own world—death, or some cataclysm confronting everything. This is true: there is always, and especially now, death and the end of things. But what has religion to say about the world's continuing? The world is continuing: not individuals, but there is (so far) some sort of continuance in marriage, children, society, and so on. Religious language has said little about all this; leaving the area open to either vagueness or conformity. It is another of the odd paradoxes of religion that only after thousands of years, with the world now on the edge of a literal destruction, is it beginning to be asked religiously what can be done about its continuing.

VI

44

THE sort of understanding that is being described is to do with a person's freedom to hold himself between opposites; of his belief both that this is possible and, if done, that there is a correlation between this and what works in the world: that these paradoxes are seen, and held, in the first place by a sort of commitment in the dark; and are continued by a process of facing whatever turns up, which is difficult but perhaps man's only freedom.

45

Marriage is a commitment, process, that in practical terms is a means to all this: two people entrusting themselves to and trying to live out some polarity not just within themselves (though this is involved) but in relationship. Marriage is, first, a recognition of this basic human need: alone, humans may have the illusion of freedom but not the means of it; they experience themselves alien in an absurd and determined world. There is in marriage an experience of a break from the past of loneliness and compulsion into a new reality of being faced with another person; of being free to do something, be something, with them. But more than this there is perhaps for the first time the experience of one's own projections on to another; which become recognisable now (formerly they seemed just helplessness) because the other that they are projected on to is faced and lived with. For in marriage it is not only that one has to come to terms with the desires and compulsions of another but, which is more difficult, with one's own—marriage inevitably confronting one with this; the matter of love being, in the first place, something of a projection, and it being this loved one, oneself, that is sometimes glimpsed and recognised. And so in the facing of these things (or not) is the possibility of the growth (or not) of freedom, not only in the relationship but in oneself. This is an enormous area that religious language has hardly touched: and psychological language though describing it theoretically has not put it in such a way that it has the force of religion—something that in ordinary life there is the self-evident truth of. That this is a proper area for religious language is because the old stories, images, do not have power any more; what does have power (authority) is the observation of the way things work —this is what people are interested in. This area is above all religious because it is to do with a way of looking at the world which is not moralistic nor exhortatory (the perversion of stories and images) but which just states what the world is like and then leaves it to the person who listens and observes to do what he likes with this.

46

In Freudian terms (as it were) marriage is a break from what one has been formed into by ancestors, parents, society—a break from a condition in which there was no working of freedom because the ego had no space (polarity) within the forces inside or outside it. A marriage is chosen, happens, in the course of growing up. Something is built—at first as a result perhaps of compulsions from the past (even if the need to make a break from them) but also, because the new thing is now there, giving a chance to be free of them. What makes a marriage—what makes a person fall in love, choose, commit himself—is often in the first place to do with the past: what a person needs, feels, and either had or had not got, he often projects, imagines, on to someone in the present; trying to repeat it, hopelessly, or find again what never existed. So long as he was in the past (with parents, background, and so on) there was nothing whereby his needs and compulsions could be faced: but when he marries, though he marries in some sense still for the need of the past (the return to it; living again some pattern of, or reaction to, childhood) he is faced with someone who in fact is not of the past

—not of his parents, of himself at all—but separate; who, being now with him however, joined, faces him with the truth of his needs, projections. Thus in marriage there is immediately both this achievement and this tension: the finding that one is not alone and is free, but also the discovery that what one is with is often a projection of oneself; and the fact that one is forced to face this and not the person one had imagined. And the other person experiences this too. In psychiatry, this sort of recognition is expected and still alarming: in marriage, the normal ground on which these things are seen, the two people are on their own, neither with much understanding of what is happening. It is here, on ground which is religious because it is to do with love, growth, freedom, that religion should have something to say but hasn't.

47

In Jungian terms (as it were) two people have fallen in love by the projection of unconscious contents on to each other; each person accepting what the other has projected so that there is a sort of marriage within the unconscious, as a dream. But the marriage is a fact. Then—in a home, routine, the thing solid, existent— the people are faced with the rejection of their dreams: just through daily life, in time, the other person is known not as imagined but something separate. It is this that is alarming: the people are not only now on their own again and helpless, each not only locked in a daily situation with a stranger, but each faced with the return of his own shadow—all the stronger since it has been glimpsed (both in the other person being not what one thought and in this one's own helplessness)—though it is not yet recognised as such, there is just pain. This sort of experience in marriage is too commonplace to need examples: in societies nowadays where marriage is not a social but personal commitment (most western societies) the experience seems almost universal: people fall in love, marry; after a time are faced with crack-up or battle, or at the best a blind acceptance of routine: this is the stuff of plays, novels; some failure at the heart of man, a loneliness, a modern tragedy. This is countered in popular jargon by advice about tolerance, mutual partnership, seeing the other person's point of view, and so on; but this sort of exhortation always misses the point, which is that a person finds himself incapable of being tolerant, understanding; finds himself in rage and despair. For the trouble at this stage is in himself: the return of his own unconscious means he is again helpless and this time more desperately, since he has had, and lost, his hope of imagined freedom. (The *anima/animus* can be a source of wonder, hope, only when its projection is accepted; this does not last; and when lost it is a source of bitterness and despair.) So that in this situation there is no answer, no possibility of freedom, except in the person recognising himself for what he is and, on his own, coming to terms with this. Marriages do endure without much freedom, even with hope; probably depending on what courage and hope have been given to people by their own families and their past: also there is a strength in fitting to a social framework however dead. But for real freedom—the possibility of growth, the escape from the power of heredity or conformity or simply luck—there has to be this recognition of the forces in oneself, of one's projections, of other people's projections on oneself; the bearing of all this with some application, effort; at first often in the dark but in the hope (as Jungians would say) that a new Self—and thus a new sort of marriage—will be born. This sort of understanding involves the idea, as always, that it is not possible for this sort of growth to be forced, achieved directly: but what is possible is for the negative things to be faced (the existence of the projections; unconscious; helplessness) and to be accepted, suffered, even in love; and then, in time, the growth happens of itself, almost unnoticed as a process of nature. And the importance of marriage in this sort of understanding is that the actual polarity of marriage—two people faced with one another intimately and continuously— is not only the means of bringing these forces to where they can be confronted even if in alarm (the power of destruction in marriage) but also the means of alleviation; means whereby just by facing the projected and returned images quite a new reality—new people and a new marriage—can grow. Although in a sense this is done by the person on his own, it is marriage that has enabled him to do it: an individual can do it formally and clinically as it were but marriage is a natural means. It is almost impossible for a person literally alone to see manifestations of his own unconscious; the other person in a marriage at least finds it easy enough to tell him of these. And in spite of the alarm, the bearing of bewilderment for a time, there is this hope in just the bringing of things to consciousness. For the discovery of the Self is not something that happens all in the dark; nor is nothing known until everything happens at once. There is even, with this sort of consciousness, the ability to pay some attention to the commonplace exhortations that were earlier useless. A person can, with the recognition of projections, listen to what the other person has to say, recognise something about his own inadequacies; and each time he does this there will be some growth of Self—even the glimpse of a new kind of marriage. These efforts, glimpses, of love (the reality of the other person) are, when observed and done, evidence for the growth and make it possible. This sort of thing is known in practice; only difficult to say or remember.

48

In religious language marriage was spoken of once as mostly a matter of church and society: as far as persons were concerned it was not very important, an arrangement for help and comfort. This was inevitable in an age when man was not self-conscious; in which religious hope was in the expectation of the end of the world or a future one; in which religious understanding was a commitment to a belief in the stories about these things or later an obedience to the rules into which they had been transmuted. In this situation man worked out the projections and rejections of his unconscious in the outside world without much recognising them: he loved, achieved, created when his commitment (belief) was true (when his projections were, or seemed, accepted): when they were not (when the belief was returned and became dead rules and impossibilities) he destroyed when he felt destructive and indulged in self-hatred and asceticism when he felt despair. In a sense this worked: people's projections were faced, dealt with, in the outside world: men fought, killed, ravaged cities: occasionally became saints with heroic powers for peace. Women stayed at home, dreamed; sometimes became witches. There was a sort of free hand for evil in this condition —people burned and murdered (even the religious) in a sort of blindness, not knowing anything about, not asking even, why they were doing this in the name of love. But there was also in some sense a free hand for good. Men who had projected parts of themselves on to God and the devil—and fallen in love with God and believed they could defeat the devil—in fact were able to live as if this were true (and thus it was true); lived with a love and an intensity which for self-conscious people are scarcely possible now, though this is still sometimes experienced and is effective. All this has changed (there is now self-consciousness) together with the stories and images not being so passionately believed in: man has just altered, grown, even if his understanding has not kept pace: he is no longer able to feel things like this, no longer able to project his unconscious and make it real—except in depersonalisation and destruction. There has been enough evidence about this in the last thirty years. There is the necessity now for him to accept back consciously his own projections; to face them and to come to terms, with difficulty, within himself. All this is happening at a time in history when (because) in the most symbolic and real form man can no longer afford his outward projections: the world has become too dangerous—man's power has become too dangerous—for men to get away with it; with getting their hatreds out by hating others, with despairing of reality by despairing of themselves: there is now the chance of a total despair and total destruction. Perhaps the world for two thousand years has been too dangerous for this: this was what was being said two thousand

84

years ago, in fact—that man must face in himself his projections (the beam in his own eye) not only the evil but also the good (the kingdom within him); all questions of religion having to be accepted back into his own condition, his own actions. But it has taken till now to see this, being faced as we are with the necessity of seeing it; and also, providentially, with the conceivable means of dealing with it; not only our technology but the insights of modern religious prophets.

49

As far as marriage is concerned—in the old state of affairs marriage worked in a sense (in the way everything worked) so long as the stories, images, were truly felt, believed in: there were good marriages according to the quality of the belief and bad marriages according to the hypocrisy: but it was still mainly luck: in this as in everything else man was largely helpless even if the world (the end of the world or a future one) had meaning. And when the stories became less and less felt and there was nothing much except the perversion of rules and literalness then marriage became specifically a matter of convention: what had once been seen as vital in the social context of salvation and the ends of things was now, still socially, seen in the context of man having to preserve a lonely dignity; woman having to inflate him in this rôle; and religion being a matter of keeping organised two people who were separate. This was achieved in some sense by the very separation of masculine and feminine worlds: men did get power and self-justification on their own; women likewise; each world was kept going in its own dream, its own onesidedness. Husband and wife by these conventions seldom faced one another (few people did); projections were not seen and growth, consciously, was not possible. All this continued (with obvious exceptions) along with everything else till the time came (has come) when this began to be not only stultifying but dangerous: the lonely and unilateral existence of men and women in not facing themselves and reality and in using convention, society, as a means of avoiding this was not only resulting in a metaphorical deadness but in literal crack-up; a tearing of each other apart in marriage, a feverishness and destructiveness of energy. It was then (is now) that there is some realisation of marriage (along with everything else) being something that can no longer drift in the dark: man has to come to terms with it—not only for its own sake but as a means of coming to terms with everything. For by facing marriage (masculine and feminine) and whatever it confronts him with, it is possible for a man to alter himself and thus to deal with the world. It is about these things that little is said in religion; and yet about which people nowadays are mysteriously and religiously interested. People do feel experience here as something religious; they are married in church: they feel

this about almost nothing else. Thus from all sides—the
need of man to know himself and marriage as a means
of doing this; the fact that old religious language has
hardly anything to say about this but that this is recognisably a religious question—what is shown is that a
new kind of religious language is necessary and also
possible.

50

There is a rôle to be played in marriage by the outside
world, by society: the known conventions are still that
which together with trust give freedom, space to move
within. But the rôle of society once was both a means of
forcing marriage and an escape from it; both of which
prevented freedom. The proper rôle of society (the outside world) is to be as it were in parallel: to give some
area in which a person can achieve separate identity,
function, work; but now, because marriage is being faced
on the other parallel (pole) ensuring the freedom of
both the person and the marriage. For there are other
paradoxes here—that although it is through the commitment of marriage that a person learns to be free,
subsistent; also, in order to be truly committed he has
in some sense to be this (subsistent) all the time—or
there is nothing to be committed with. This can be done,
outwardly (with the inner business of marriage and projections) where men and women exist, work, act on their

87

own. They bring what they have gained there into marriage; to some extent give it up there, but at least have had it to give. And then, having given it in order to be more together (themselves) go out again—to be solitary, creative, for comfort even. This goes on of course apart from marriage: but the point is that unless there is some sort of polarity even here—the outside effort, toughness, and the inner learning, humility—both become hazy, both achievement and self knowledge are almost impossible. A man in particular may need some identity, strength, apart from marriage; it being perhaps his responsibility more than woman's to be the agent of change, to be solitary and committed enough to be the conscious carrier of paradoxes which are change's methods. But the woman, still, has to be free enough to accept this. So that in a true marriage there has to be this commitment without clinging, this dedication with respect, this recognition of a unity within which there are separate identities. This sort of language has images of theology: it should not be difficult for religious people to understand, if they used it about this sort of subject which they do not.

51

Also the old theological language talked about marriage as something which, if it had been faithfully entered into, was indissoluble; and this too should be understandable.

Once people have entered into the business of coming to terms with themselves, their projections, other people, and so on, then, if they turn their backs on this, they are turning their backs on a chance of growth and understanding; and in this sense the marriage cannot be got away from, it is a point beyond which, except by facing whatever is there, further progress cannot be made. So that even if on the surface the marriage is broken the people concerned are committing themselves in this way to the break; to a haunting by it. All this depends of course on the qualification that such a marriage should have been faithfully entered into—whatever this means, which is fortunately almost anything. The church in theory has been sensible about this: saying that a marriage not faithfully entered into is void—which is true. But in practice the church has as always defined the question of faith so closely that it has begged the whole question of what faith might be—and thus denied it. Faith is properly, in this sort of language, something which can only be known by the people concerned: others can state opinions, but their authority will rest on the self-evidence of their case—their putting it in front of other people and leaving it for them to do as they like with —and not upon powers of persuasion. There are so-called marriages, then, that can be ended thus, in nullity, because they have never begun. And there are also marriages which, even though entered into faithfully (the people themselves believing faithfully) may still end in divorce (again fortunately) if the people have to sidestep the business of religion—that of facing illusions and coming to terms with themselves and other people. All this has to be done freely: the facts (the way things seem to work) can be offered, stated; but it is the people concerned, if anything is to be religious, who have to choose. But what does seem to be involved here that those who want to embark on the business of learning, growing, do want at some stage to make this sort of commitment—not only a jump in the dark but a determination and promise to stick to something there—which, if achieved, is marriage. There has to be commitment because nothing else will carry people over the difficulties and bewilderment before the new things (people and relationship) grow. And most people do want to commit themselves like this—want passionately to make the jump, stick to it—because they know, even unconsciously, that this is their means of growth. They want to pledge their joy and intensity in the present (the falling in love; the projections) as a means of carrying on in the future; in the faith that if they do this then both they and the world are such that this will be justified. There is some recognition here of what is meant by eternity: what is felt, known, in the present, being staked as worthwhile for ever. This love is what nowadays people still know; and is their contact with religion.

VII

52

CHILDREN, the result of relationship (marriage) are both the reality and the symbol of that which grows—two people committing themselves perhaps in the dark; recognising their helplessness, need of love; in the hope (faith) or even ignorance that something new will grow; something to which (where) love can be given freely; theirs and yet quite separate from them.

53

Children, especially young, are the chance that man has to alter the world; to create something not just in the sense of procreation but in being consciously free to turn human nature into something better or something worse. Psychologists know this: that the characters of human beings are formed in their early years—not character in the way of what type of person they are (as if there were some type that everyone should attain to) but in the way of whether they are healthy or sad of whatever type they happen to be: that they are formed into this by the influences of people around them, above all or almost exclusively by their parents.

While in later life it is very difficult for character to change, in childhood it is receptive to whatever is given. In fact all people who look after children know this — that they have an enormous power for good and evil in their hands. It is perhaps this also that frightens people. For it is in this area above all (perhaps together with that of marriage) that people both know and yet refuse to know something fundamentally; both know that in bringing up of children they have possibly their only power to control human nature and alter the world and yet they (and religion too) keep on talking as if there were other and more important ways — technology, politics, and so on — and as if children could be left to customary disciplines and platitudes.

54

Psychologists say that a child's welfare depends on love: that if a child is given love it prospers and if it is not it does not. But how is this love known, and how to give it? The opposite of love is power — that which often in the name of love is really the satisfaction of needs — the attempt at control and even destruction. In all life but especially with children because they are vulnerable there is this masking of power in the name of love (few people now call it power; if they do, it is perhaps exorcised) and sometimes there is genuine difficulty in distinguishing giving from need. Psychologists talk of the difficulties of loving for a person who himself has not received love; he is helpless with the demands of his own needs. For him, there is almost the impossibility of giving love (especially to children) until he has come to terms with himself—until he has recognised his needs and projections in relationship. But if he does this, what he learns is that by this breaking of his own past of heredity and lovelessness and power he will not only be able to give to his children but enable them to give in their turn—without what he had to go through. This, for most children, is the most important gift in the world—a sort of redemption from some original suffering. The old language of religion had a lot to say about this; very little now about what each parent can do for his child.

55

The paradox of all love, and especially that of children, is that love, truly, is something that both cares for (and has authority with) the loved person and yet leaves him free. This is a definition of love: it is either felt, experienced, or it isn't. There is something important in this conception of love and of the difference between love and power (what does not care for a person but wants to control him) for the understanding not only of people but of the old language about God: and although this language may not now be so relevant, what it refers to is still vital for an understanding of the way things work. What most people object to in the old language about God is that God was supposed to be all-powerful and all-good in a world of suffering; such a concept of God, they say, meant that he permitted suffering and so could not be good—or more likely did not exist. The christian answer to this has always been (and is; only the old language has to be translated into the new) that God cares for man but has created man free (man has free-will in a world of laws); that this is the highest form of creation man can imagine because it is a creation of love; and that for God to interfere and revoke man's freedom would be to destroy the point of man and indeed of love. All that God could do, christians say, because he cared about suffering, was himself to partake of it; which he did. (In the new language, it is man's experience of love that it makes other things seem worthwhile.) Non-christians still say that the experiment is not worthwhile: but they say this from a horror of the world rather than of God, not much thinking he exists; and it is this fact that it is not disgust with God (as it were) but disgust with the world that makes people irreligious that is relevant here again to a new religious language. For what these people are objecting to is just the way the world works: and against them—though truly christian people are passionate that the world is good—there can be no argument logically. All that can be put to the irreligious is—What then is their own experience of love? If they have experience of love as what is freely given and what leaves the other person free is it not in fact such as to make other things (even suffering) at least bearable (the idea of it)? Or if they have not this experience of love, can it be talked about? This is difficult, again, because the horror of suffering is real; but such is still people's experience. This is an area where the new language and the old come together with experience; where perhaps each is not intelligible (attainable) without the other.

56

(The facts of suffering are so appalling that there is little that can be said about them; only things done, and perhaps suffered. The explanation that suffering is a corollary of evil and that evil (or the chance of it) is a necessary corollary of man's freedom is all right as a theory but useless in the face of actual suffering. This is an area which words cannot touch directly; only observations can be made from the periphery. It seems true that people who believe in God do not usually find their belief shaken by suffering: the ages of faith were those in which men lived very close to suffering, and it is now, when suffering is mostly hidden, that there is the idea that it makes God appalling. Thus horror at God seems to come from the mind and not from experience. Also it seems untrue that people are frightened into religion: in an irreligious age they can be frightened into bitterness as easily. An understanding of suffering seems to run parallel to that of faith, together with some understanding of reality; but still not in words, only experience. Ivan Karamazov, appalled by the suffering of children, was articulate and wanted to turn his back on experience. Alyosha, equally appalled, was inarticulate but did not. That is, he helped suffering children. This is perhaps a burden of suffering—that there is only something to be done about it. But when this is accepted, not rejected, there seems to be faith —also love. This is relevant to the question of the relation of parents to children because parents know terror of the innocent suffering—and the necessity of their own love.)

57

In the love for a child, young child, by its parents, there is at first not much demand for the child to be free: the child is wholly dependent on the mother and the mother is dependent emotionally on the child: through these early stages the love is as compulsive and unselfconscious as perhaps it was in the days of parents' falling-in-love: people just want, need one another; exist inwards in a mutually nourishing dream. Then at a certain stage (perhaps from the beginning) the child makes demands on the mother that the mother cannot properly meet; the mother starts wanting the child to be something that it cannot be. There are not only the impossible demands on the mother's time, the resentment by the child when the mother does not meet these, but the recognition, even, that it is not proper they should be met; even the recognition, in a sense, that the child should have resentment. These are the early instances of the paradox, polarities, that haunt the whole of love—without which the free giving and receiving of love is inexplicable; and it being necessary to explain this now, man having grown inescapably into self-consciousness. For love is not always the giving to a person of what he wants and certainly not the giving of what a person himself wants to give—it is some regard, trust, passion, quite apart from all this; some holding of a balance within which, and not at extremes, love will grow and be kept from what will harm it. With parents and their children the extremes are obvious: children are harmed equally by the neglect and over-control of their parents. By neglect children are unable to find an identity both because they are not shown an example of it and have nothing to exercise themselves against; by over-control they are also made helpless and afraid, even by the solicitous and suffocating worry that is sometimes called love and is not. But there are more paradoxes, polarities, here; and of increasing complexity. As soon as a child begins to grow away from its mother just in the course of things—the mother not properly having the time and it being bad for the child if she had—then, when the child resents this, the mother has both to care and not to care—to care because if she does not then the child will know its resentment is justified and will be desolate (and be harmed, not being able to bear this); and not to care because if she cares too much (or, in this language, if she cares without not caring) then it is she who will not be able to bear it and will answer the demands of the child but this time falsely, not because of need but through threats and despair; and this will not only be to her own detriment (her own resentment; though even if this is recognised the child might still be freed) but, resentment usually being unconscious and self-justified, to the detriment of the child. For there is a sense here in which the child too when it makes demands on the mother at the same time both does and does not want the mother to respond —does because the need or resentment is genuine; and does not because there is something in the child even then that recognises (as it were, unconsciously) what is the proper course of its growth; that only by experiencing this first sort of solitariness can it grow; that a mother's preventing this would mean its condemnation to lasting childishness. These are the kinds of thing however obscure which mothers and fathers do in fact experience with children: parents (people with the possibilities of creating, altering life) are faced with whole sets of phenomena and choices which are not describable in any other way: if they are seen in terms of extremes there is damage visibly, but if in terms of paradox, polarity, then there is the rightness of the results — children do flourish and grow if parents preserve both care and necessary freedom. Fathers and mothers know this; but have no language (except poetry, art) for it and thus to deal with it. The sort of language wanted is, as has been said, a way of thinking, talking, in which what matters is the state of mind when faced with facts and decisions rather than an attempt to argue the possible rightness of what is decided — the state of mind being to do with holding consciously the paradoxical demands of a situation and not worrying too much about action (though there has to be action) in the hope, knowledge, that just by doing this, holding paradoxes, whatever is done will be right. Otherwise, action will have been decided, argued, compulsively. In the care of children there are of course innumerable instances in which action is explicit — practical care, nourishment and so on — and these are as necessary for love as anything. But in questions about what might be proper apart from this (common enough in all families) what matters is not the effort to judge where there are no criteria but the effort towards what should be faced and trusted by the person judging — even of himself. It is this that needs an understanding, language, that is religious. Religion once had its stories about these things; not now practicalities about life, growth, children.

58

As a child grows into adolescence these situations become more pronounced and almost farcical: what Freud called the Oedipus complex being a name for what most families experience—just that as children grow up there is usually some conflict between fathers and sons and in a way between mothers and daughters: there are ties between mothers and sons and between fathers and daughters which, however good, can be destructive: and finally if there are none of these things then perhaps this is the most dangerous state of all because it means that people may be incapable of almost any feeling whatever. Thus the things noticed in the Oedipus theories are both neurotic and yet necessary; it being impossible for anyone to make sense of them except by recognising both aspects at once—which is what Freud did implicitly but not explicitly. In practice it is only by a mother having a continuing tie of love with a son that the son will know about love and to give it in his turn; but it is also only by this tie being in some sense broken that he will be able to direct love where it should be—towards his own wife and family eventually and not backwards on the mother, towards impotence, promiscuity or homosexuality. Similarly with fathers and daughters—if there is not a genuine tie then the daughter will not learn about love (and the father may learn later what it is not); but also, if this tie is not broken, then the daughter may only be able to love someone who represents a father and thus remain lastingly childish. This sort of thing is observable in the other sets of relationships—those between fathers and sons and mothers and daughters. If there is no kind of rivalry (as well as authority) between fathers and sons then the sons have no chance to prove themselves and thus break away from the father's domination; but if there is total enmity and no authority the sons remain infants because of this too—perpetually alone in adolescent rebellion. And the father may even welcome this: willing, in his own loneliness, the fruitlessness of his sons and thus himself. Between mothers and daughters the daughter's need of the mother is more practical; but daughters (and later their husbands) who stay at the mercy of mothers (mothers-in-law) are jokes. These sorts of situation are the stuff of life for most people: they are what families worry, argue, fight over; do their best with and sometimes destroy one another. But nearly always (because this is what people are accustomed to) they think and talk in terms of either one extreme or the other—either to keep their children stifled or to give up responsibility; either to treat their parents as models or mock them as clowns. Often they do these one after the other, blowing hot and cold; but this is the opposite of holding two attitudes together. To follow an extreme is to be unconsciously compelled: to hold paradoxes is a conscious effort and choice.

Families know this. What works—what makes children free and caring—is the ability of parents to be free and caring themselves; both to love, be tied, and yet to be wholly subsistent in some different area of identity.

59

The purpose of all this is not to say what should be a way of bringing up children but something about the way of thinking, talking, that seems the only way to make sense of it: a way that is in fact glimpsed by everyone dealing with things like love, birth, growth, death; but about which we find it almost impossible to talk nowadays so sophisticated are we after the death of images. We have reached a stage at which we seem able to make sophisticated statements only about things that are trivial, useless or even destructive: for the rest we find ourselves at the mercy of people saying trivial, useless or destructive things. There was once a point to all this: fundamental statements had mostly been made at extremes; they had exhorted people to be moral, obedient and so on, according to the predispositions of the writer or speaker; they had threatened people with punishment if they were not. Because this was destroying man's freedom, his necessary consciousness, it was in fact moral when a generation (most young generations) came along to try to make a nonsense of it; to reduce exhortations to the matter of the compulsions of the people making them, to mock extremists for being inhuman. In doing this they (the young) preserved something vital of freedom: but also (perhaps because they were, are, something of extremists themselves, having so little hope) there resulted from this a danger of the most inhuman extremism of all—one which flourished (and flourishes) just in this terror that in truth everything might be ridiculous. For most people not only cannot bear that this might be so but at some level do not believe it: so, when faced either with old generations demonstrating by their behaviour that everything is ridiculous or with young generations proving by their cleverness that it is—people, some people, both young and old, tend to go to an extreme so powerful that it alone perhaps cannot seem ridiculous—something which in its inhumanity is even satanic. It is about this sort of extremism that there has been enough evidence in the last thirty years. But the point is that we know this now; have experience of it: we cannot go back to an archaic simple-mindedness and are terrified of a total inhumanity. Yet we cannot go on for ever not being able to say anything about love, hope, truth, freedom—except in terms which we find embarrassing. We have got to say something to our children. The reason for this is not moral but one of danger: nowadays when we try to be prophetic we need not presuppose a future heaven or hell, the dangers of hell and the necessity to try for heaven are here on earth and immediate. They are in man's consciousness; conceivable control.

60

The point of marriage, children, families, in this sense, is, as has been said, that these (and we know it) are man's chances to alter the world—in marriage perhaps himself and with children the future. And it is in this that there is in fact a true religious movement of our time; men and women working and talking in this way—not only families but counsellors, psychologists, workers in clinics, and so on—talking not in extremes but in paradoxes; looking at each case in terms of evidence and not of rules and projections; recognising that health, goodness, depend on a person learning something for and about himself, and not in accepting an imposed rigidity. These people are not talking about morals, they are talking about facts. They are saying—'This is the way the world works; seems to work: we can tell you this but we cannot compel or even persuade you; we can just offer you knowledge to do as you like with.' They are saying—'Evil is discernible from what people do, the results of this; it is not a matter of moral judgement: if people grow up in a certain way they do seem to hate, destroy, want to kill one another and themselves: if they grow up in another way they do not: so—make your choice.' The people who talk like this are the truly religious. And against them are all the people who think this sort of thing somewhat ludicrous—who think they need not learn anything of love and growth and death, who do not want to. The distinction between these two sorts of people is vital. And here the old apparent enemies, the cynics and the bigots, are on the same side: together they depend on rigidity, separateness, man's helplessness; they even depend on each other for hate: they are against any concept of fluidity, relationship, change. Between birth and somewhere in the twenties or thirties human beings are capable of change: they are often capable of little else, but after this they lose it. During this time they are moving towards either freedom or helplessness—to something flourishing or already in the form of death. And during this time everyone around a person influences him; by omission even if, as is usual, there is hardly any contact—this itself being a movement towards death, growth depending on contact. People do not often acknowledge this because they feel such relationship to be impertinence; and it can be, if compulsive. But it is the definition of the sort of contact spoken of here that it is without compulsion, without exhortion even; it is just the being of one person towards another; the one person knowing, holding, something which the other perhaps has not got but which he can, if he likes, ask for. There is no compulsion in this; just something more difficult —the effort of a person to be this sort of thing himself—

a carrier of life rather than of death—and to show this in his actions. It is because of the difficulty of this rather than because of respect that people nowadays shy away from it. The demand is to let others grow by growing oneself; and in this one often appears self-contradictory. One has to appear a person of total hope and none; of limitless confidence and impotence. As has been said—All this is of course just what the christian religion has always implied and is always turning itself away from.

VIII

61

THE person who feels the necessity of growth, change, tries to allow this to happen where he can influence it—himself, people around him, family, children—and in his larger surroundings over which he has not so much control; but here his attitude of trying to hold opposites in himself may appear from a distance disconcertingly to be facing both ways: for when confronted by people at extremes—the extremely bigoted or the extremely sceptical—in work, society, the world, and so on—the only means by which such a person can in fact remain consistent is by appearing self-contradictory. Thus it has always been the accusation of bigots and sceptics against the truly religious that they are trying to have the best of both worlds—which they are—this (the comprehension of everything) being the business of religion.

62

One of the most ludicrous apparent conflicts nowadays between bigots and sceptics—ludicrous because so fierce and only apparent because they are on the same side—is the one about sexual morality. Here the attitude of the bigots is well known: sexual practice is wrong except in marriage. Authority for their attitude is sometimes claimed from natural law but, because there is little evidence for this in nature, more often from divine revelation—what is reported of the words of Christ. But this is almost the only area in which this divine revelation is taken literally; bigots pay little attention, that is, to other divine recommendations. This is the whole case against christian bigots—not that their recognition of a few of Christ's words is untrue but that they recognise only a tiny proportion of all that Christ said; and by paying earnest and passionate attention to the part and scarcely any to the whole (which sometimes seems to be in opposition to the part) they not only pervert the whole but even the part that they pay attention to. It is true, that is, that every now and then Christ said that fornication and adultery were wrong; but what he also said (and what his whole life and the whole story of the bible seem to be about) was that this sort of wrongness (whatever this may mean; which from Christ's words and actions is complicated) did not seem on its own much to matter. What did matter much more was something like, for instance, being a religious bigot—even specifically in the matter of sexual morality. The real sin was to be thinking that other people's sexual doings should automatically come up against one's own active judgement; it was this, in the story in the New Testament, that made Christ angry.

But nowadays the bigots are obviously on the defensive. What is more important, because it is in favour, is the attitude of the extreme sceptics: which is that there is something magical and healing in sex; that sex is not a commitment to love but a means for it; or something apart from love, both inside and outside marriage. In this sort of attitude sexuality takes on something of the mystical aura once held by revelation; there is supposed to be something ultimate for the personality about technique, orgasm, satisfaction, and so on. For evidence, sceptics appeal to experience; but although it is difficult to get evidence in this sort of area (difficult to be honest with oneself as well as to learn honestly from others) people do seem to know, when pressed, that the extreme pursuit of sex for its own sake does not find love nor indeed much human contact (it may at some stage in a person's life produce the chance of it, but this is different) but rather their opposite, a loneliness; that the achievement of better technique and more successful orgasm (though at certain times in people's lives the attempt at this may be necessary, and rewarding) does not in fact result in fulfilment but in something impersonal and almost neutral. Even the people who make the mystical claims for sex in fact know this: the only people who do not seem to be the bigots, who still seem to fear it is only marvellous and thus has to be controlled by appeal to law and not to experience. There is evidence about all this, again, in art—in which there is honesty apart from self-deception. It is almost impossible to imagine a good play or novel, for instance—good in the sense of being recognisably good as art—that denied the destructive results of the extreme pursuit of sexuality: denied that it seemed to be driving to ever further extremes, moving towards inhumanity and cruelty or at least to states the opposite of which were intended—men becoming more womanish, that is, and women more masculine. The absurdity of these sorts of extremes is that people who live by them know that they have little to do with what is pretended: what is supposed to be liberating, life-giving, is in fact enslaving and perverse. What is found, that is, is that sexuality never is just on its own: it is either balanced by something of its opposite—fidelity, honesty, even sacrifice—or it brings with it deception, despair; goes into sadism and destruction; extreme forms of writing about this even describing it specifically. Pornography often contains a philosophy of life in which the world is described as logically deceptive and brutal; even the theory (and this is important) that brutality is the only way to make real the concepts of order, single-mindedness and consistency (de Sade).

What drives bigots to their putting of extreme taboos and threats around sex perhaps is, as well as not knowing about it, just some such concern for order, single-mindedness—some idea of what the world ought to be like if everyone were in a state of static harmony. If there were such a state (whatever this might mean) bigots might be right: sex would be confined to marriage because this would ensure security for harmony by preventing jealousy and aggression. But all this is an opinion about an ideal; something perhaps always to be carried as true about an ideal and even consciously to be striven for; but as far as the state of things as they are is concerned not untrue but largely irrelevant. The world, and people, never are in a state of harmony: they are struggling, groping, learning. In this state it is not incorrect to talk about the ideals of love and marriage so long as one does not imagine one is saying what is to be done about love and marriage—what is to be done in the circumstances, that is, to achieve anything approaching harmony. This has to be something not to be willed directly (this fails) but in the area of man's special freedom. In fact people have drives, difficulties, fears, that are not touched by the exhortations towards ideals: but if not talked about at all they remain in the unconscious and fester, so that something has to be done (said) about them but always in some other terms than of just denying them; understood in some language of what is possible. The point of this is that it is the people who preach an ideal moral rectitude who in fact make an approach to moral rectitude almost impossible: what seems to happen to them is much the same as what seems to happen to those who preach an extreme moral anarchy—what supposedly guards tenderness and liveliness results in a sort of death; even in the odd reversal of rôles such as is seen with the libertines—that of pious men becoming increasingly feminine and pious women increasingly masculine. (This is one of the true moral problems of this time; a sort of emasculation, loss of authority, both amongst the pious and impious, in sexuality not as love-making but as the relations between men and women.) It is the argument against the moralists, then, that it is they, together with the libertines, who are turning us all into zombies, sadists, voyeurs, and so on—the drives, difficulties, coming out somewhere and nowadays in all forms of half-lights— and not they who are preventing this. And the driving force behind both extremists is the same—a lack of trust in relationship; a compulsion to try to impose a sort of stasis, death-wish, upon what is living and fluid; an effort to treat men as ultimately perfect or rather logically consistent when they are, in growth, neither. And what prevents this sort of perversion, and is the true morality, is just a recognition of this growth; of this as man's true function.

It would seem obvious that humans, as everything else living, change, grow: that this is their function apart from which they cannot be talked about; growth consisting both of a sort of spontaneity, letting-go, and of certain containments and even sacrifice. Sexually these opposites are connected from the beginning with the paradoxical situation of parent-child relationship. A person deprived in his early years of love, security, may have no means later of experiencing human contact other than sexuality (even at the beginning through what might be called quite loveless sexuality) and this, however destructive (or not) at the time, might yet be a means of learning something about human contact; of re-living, even destructively, something of the pain and fears of earlier years but this time because less helpless with a chance of growing out of it—even into health and love. And someone brought up in early years with apparent comfort and security may yet find themselves remaining peculiarly childish and for growth may have to risk something of a commitment to insecurity (spontaneity). These are situations in which sensuality, in this sense, may be necessary: not right (though what goes with it—honesty and courage, deception and betrayal, and its results—may be right; or wrong) but just there, inevitable; and going on through the whole of life. A way of thinking is required in which a proper demand upon, or function of, a person can be talked about as well as right and wrong: or rather in which wrongness, sometimes, can be seen in the instance not so much to matter—it being in the situation anyway, and possibly right in a sense if known, admitted, and something is done. In these sorts of situation there seems to be something built into human nature that makes talk at either extreme essentially ridiculous: human beings seem to be born with opposites, and the demands of opposites, within them: as if they have to put up always with an intricate balance, the experiences of spontaneity and discipline, acceptance and dissolution, finding themselves and losing themselves, simultaneously —for the sake of growth. It is as if people were born with the impossibilities of a perfectly satisfiable sensuality (amongst other things) and a perfectly satisfying chastity—and they have to do what they can with these. The only way in which fidelity makes sense is if it is something given freely (conceivable it should be broken); the only way in which sexuality makes sense is if it is seen, achieved, together with something parallel— austerity, even sacrifice. This is not to say that there is no such thing as a satisfying sexuality, but to make the more difficult statement that when, of course, there is, this will be in quite a different area—that of love.

The matter of sexuality is important because now with the break-up of other sorts of masculine and feminine endeavour (men going out to fight and conquer the world; women running homes with fourteen children) it is one of the areas left in which people on their own, men and women, try to prove themselves—young men especially perhaps needing some such risk with masculinity for the sake of freedom, breaking out—and perhaps women thanking them for this. But the point is that this is an area in which this sort of thing never really quite works—or only works if, as has been said, there is recognised something of its opposite. And in fact people nowadays do have this complex sort of knowledge: bigots know the impossibility of trying to impose moral rectitude by will, cynics that without any effort there is unreality and even will-to-destruction. They admit this in private; seldom in public. There the tone of bigots becomes querulous; which ruins their case, a pity, because half of it is true. This lets the sceptics stay in their own position which they know is not satisfying either. What moralists (everyone; both conservative and radicals) should be talking about now is not ideals (impossibilities) but what is possibly attainable in the sense previously described—in the way of not aiming at what is desired and out of reach but at something personal and graspable and then perhaps finding, almost unseen, that what is desired has occurred. If a person is using his will to hold on consciously to all the complexities in himself in the hope of growth, change —if he is doing what he can for love, tolerance, self-understanding, and so on—then, in the matter of sexuality (abstinence as well as satisfaction) he will probably find himself, not by will but by occurrence, in the sort of situation that the bigots might desire— being faithful, that is; this being what he finds most happy. He will have found that there are ideals because without them there is neither meaning nor freedom of movement; but also he will have found the experience that everything has to be faced in terms of itself, of what it is capable of being made into, and not directly in terms of what it should be. But what had once seemed impossible commandments may then be discovered as facts. People who do face all this (even commandments) in the hope of growth do seem to find that what they hope for happens for them—they happen not to bear false witness, that is, not to commit adultery, not to fornicate—not because they now make themselves not do these things but just because they do not want to. They will know, from experience, the sort of dissolution, loss, that goes with all this; and they will (if admitted) want something different—love. This is the most impor-tant thing about morals. As has been said, the people making most sense nowadays about marriage, children, and so on, are not talking about morals but about facts:

and similarly those who try to live out these things—to face experience and not be afraid of it—find that facts as it were are moral—human beings are such that they perhaps only properly function when they are acting morally; even that the world is such that it helps them to realise this, and to make other things happen when they do not. This does not mean that the wicked do not flourish (they do) but that, if we know enough about wickedness (and its opposite) we do not want to flourish like them. Nowadays the dangers of evil are felt too closely and frighteningly for there to be a need for morality to be imposed—and anyway, if this is tried it is no morality. Heaven and hell are observable: experience is moral.

67

What is wanted, as always, is the sort of language, way of thinking (religious) that will contain all this; that will become habitual and not a strain on reason or credulity. People feel in these terms already: feel the dangers of both bigotry and libertinism; but there is a fear nowadays of compromise—of missing the point of both. But the sort of facing both ways advocated here is different from compromise: it is comprehension; in one sense the only true liveliness because it is in recognition of the way the world works. And there again are the two sorts of people recognisable: the life carriers who by comprehension of opposites (everything) love the world enough (in spite of everything) to stake their trust on it, even on morality being discoverable by trust: and the death carriers, bigots and libertines, whose contention that morality is not discoverable in life but has to be imposed or denied comes from a dislike of life on which they cannot put their trust. Beyond this about sexuality there is almost nothing to be said: every word about it, describing it, has to be said with its opposite—it is that by which love is made and destroyed, contact is achieved and found illusory, shame is disastrous and a safeguard. It is ironic that sexual morality is almost the only form of morality about which people still make black and white state-ments—especially christians. When Christ was asked to judge a case of sexual morality—that of the woman caught in adultery—he made the one perfectly apt and significant gesture (which he used at other moments of great importance for instance at his trial) which was, to say nothing. He said nothing about the sexual morality, that is; just turned the question back against the accusers —the real matter of morality in such a situation being to do not with the woman but with them. For sexuality is perhaps one area in a person's life in which there is nothing to be said except that there are ideals, which people know and have to recognise; that there is experi-ence, from which they have to learn and do their best; and apart from this everything can be forgiven. For sexuality is not only nowadays a common ground but also always a sort of central impossibility for man; where his creative humanity meets with some extreme of impotence, where he is perhaps most like a god with not much to be done about it. It is no wonder that people have been so terrified of sex, since they know so little. It is only now, when everything can be held so consciously, that there has perhaps to be a getting over of this fear: it is again too dangerous: what has to be accepted is not only a recognition but also a compassion, tenderness, towards anything so vulnerable.

IX

68

IN the matter of power, politics, society, there is a
state of affairs which is both obviously recognised
and tacitly unadmitted—that politics is a game in
which people plot, deceive, strike spurious attitudes; yet
in which they are seriously working for the organisation
of the world. This is how politicians are seen; and why
they are held in such scorn by the young and respect by
the old—the young being hopeful and in this at least
concerned with ideals and the old being anxious and
in this at least knowing ideals don't work. But also, it
seems no better attitude towards politics has been
discovered: the theory that society can best be controlled by one group of single-minded enthusiasts given
the devotion of followers has been, for the moment in
the western world at least, exploded. By appalling trial
and error it has been recognised that single-mindedness
and devotion together with power are disastrous; that
anything, even the cynicism of a political game, is better.
But then, what matters are the game's conventions.
The world is such that there are no absolutes in matters
of power; no absolute good that is; and the best that
can be hoped for and attempted is some balancing of

forces, an arrangement whereby any too great concentration of power can be repudiated and cancelled, rather than the attempt to find some concentration and faith in it that will finally, against all the evidence, work. The reason for believing this is again just evidence: nowadays we have had enough of it.

69

The corollary to this knowledge that political fanaticism is perverted by power is not that there should just be political cynicism: what is required, as always, is some recognition of both. It is not only that extreme cynicism could not work politically—such leadership could not get power and such people would not give it (there is magic, largely unconscious, in any giving and receiving of power)—but also that cynicism seems curiously contained in fanaticism, here again extremes being alike in manifestations. An idealism about power contains a cynical contempt for people: contempt for people contains an idealisation of oneself. Totalitarianism has demonstrated this with its mixture of grandiloquence and squalor. What seems to work politically (works, that is, according to what politicians claim — that they are achieving order, progress, happiness of the greatest number, and so on) is some state of affairs, society, in which scepticism and enthusiasm, mockery and admiration, all are recognised and play their part:

a society which can never be thought to be achieved and balanced perfectly but which can be perpetually approximated to. The business of politics, that is, is not the achievement of a perfect order but the preventing of any extreme that will go against some natural growth. This is not the sort of conservatism that sees its central position in terms of the maintenance of an archaic *status quo*, but rather the tough and sometimes revolutionary activity that alone permits growth—and also, of course, a true conservatism and order.

70

The view that the world is such that such systems of counterpoise are necessary means that societies should contain recognisably reactionaries and rebels; or forces will be unconscious and therefore violent. People will be reactionaries or rebels by chance, heredity, upbringing: there will be some enmity between them and without this too a healthy society is inconceivable—there would be apathy and again neurosis. But what is necessary in this view is that these two sorts of people should not, because they feel enmity, only hate and fight; but, because of this, do something to understand one another and themselves—the very fact of what they feel (enmity) being evidence that what is demanded of them is tolerance and self-criticism as well as the passionate holding to their views. It should be taken for granted, that is, that when a person has passionate feelings he should question his righteousness and hostility—not holding passions to be wrong for without them nothing can be loved, lived—but also not holding them to be such that he should do violence (hatred) for them—though violence and hate might sometimes be necessary, but not in self-righteousness. But before such a person can judge the rightness of this sort of thing (of what to do about it) he first has to come to terms with himself (or how can he judge?) understand his own feelings, and something of the people they are directed against. It is true there is a danger here of everything being taken subjectively (together with the danger of everything being taken objectively)—passions being explained away as only an unfortunate sickness of the person who is feeling them as well as passions resulting in nothing but hatred for the person they are put upon—but this only happens if nothing is known about what to do. As always, there is no sense to be made of this sort of understanding except in terms of what to do—which is, here, to accept both sorts of attitude (subjective and objective) and then, only then, whatever is done having a chance of being right in the situation. As Christ said—the reasonable attitude is not not to have enemies but to love them; also to love oneself, which is the same thing. The wrong attitude is to cling to self-justification or self-guilt—again, the same things. The only absolutes here are words like integrity, courage;

which are apart from matters of power, but sometimes still command them.

71

In practice nowadays reactionaries and rebels are too often much the same; the reactionaries flatter the rebels and the rebels accept flattery as clowns. Both these sorts of people are committed to the projections put upon them; their triviality (sameness) is in their public image; they have notoriety but little influence in the matter of freedom, change. It is the people in the central position who in this sense have power—the ability to face either way, to choose to act according to circumstances and not to what is expected. In modern democratic politics people in the centre achieve change not only in the obvious way of being the only people who vote freely but in the way that people at extremes are always having to pay them attention; so that for all the apparent power of people at extremes (in fact the rigidity; the compulsion of the public image) it is as if they depended even for their illusion on people quite private and unknown—which in fact they do, the great merit of democratic politics. In non-democratic politics the extremists (revolutionaries) do sometimes take over; they do this violently, and violence can be a necessary forerunner to change: but violence itself is just a break-up, movement to nothingness, out of which something new, or not, can come. And after all the helplessness of blood and suffering (it is difficult to imagine extremists in power except as being driven by blood and suffering) it is again the people at the centre who have, and have had, this chance of permanent effect—not those who have compromised in alliance with the extremists but those who have worked against them for the sake of the future—determining what will in fact happen after the break-up, which will mend. Thus during periods of oppression the power of freedom (within the oppressed state at least) comes obviously to reside where in fact it always is—in private conviction, action, choice (to resist or to collaborate)—though of course this is manifested outwards and politically. And it is one of the marks of the extremists that they become so literally and symbolically involved with death; not only with war and murder but romantically in obsessions with ghosts and fear. It is also one of the experiences of people of the centre that they become involved with life and hope: seldom ready to kill for it; reluctantly to die.

72

The character of the society in which this central position can flourish is one in which there is a tacit admission even amongst so-called extremists that what matters is not one particular view of passion above all others but that people should be able to express their different views and passions without hindrance—with very important exceptions, which are to do with the prevention of cruelty, intolerance, and so on; those things that would themselves destroy freedom and thus the point of such a society. This is now in the western world admitted: the importance of such concepts as liberty, equality, justice, is not just that it is kinder of those in power to allow odd people to say a few odd things; but fundamentally that the whole health of a society depends on this; that it is the condition without which nothing can properly grow, not even the power of the most orthodox. This has been learned by the usual trial and disastrous error. But however much this is now largely accepted there is some question that would seem to be at the back of it that is not: which is —granted that by trial and error the best (happiest) kind of working of the social-political world has been found to be one in which liberty, the free play of inter-acting forces and opinions, is allowed and guarded; what reasonable inference can be made from this about the nature of the world? For the trust in liberty—the trust that if things are allowed to go their own way with just man's negative safeguardings against violence, cruelty and exploitation, then, and only then, will the world work as it should be working—all this implies some trust in the way the world works on its own (as it were); some trust in a meaning and a power for good in the world apart from man—it being man's rôle just to provide safeguards. For without trust in such a power how could man reasonably trust that it is best if there is liberty? Such an hypothesis can be ignored (can be held to be useless) but is difficult to deny. It is ignored now probably because people are suspicious of suggestions that there are powers and meanings in the world—this sort of language not only is supposed to be unscientific but has been found dangerous—it is the sort of idealism and historicism that has led to the world's disasters. But the concepts of meaning and power such as are being suggested here are different from the old dogmas of idealism and historicism; nothing is posited, imposed by man's minds on a recalcitrant world; but rather something is discovered, suggested, in and from the world. And this process is in fact scientific in that it produces hypotheses only out of what is observed; and thus these hypotheses are tentative, liable to change (though temporarily useful) according to further observations and experience. But if there are no such hypotheses then it is this that is unscientific: men do observe this trust in liberty and that it works: and hypotheses are necessary for science, since it is only by inferring something from observation that further observations and hypotheses can be made. It is thus strange that people who believe in liberty do not much question the grounds of their beliefs: and their reluctance is perhaps due to something more even than a reasonable dislike of historicism—to a dislike of religion.

What is in fact allowed into the discussion of some such hypothesis is a suggestion about God; and people do not want, again perhaps reasonably, to bring in such a concept because of all the connotations that come in with it. In this instance as in so many others what prevents a reasonable discussion about (or indeed a belief in) God is the language and behaviour of people who talk about God but in such a way as to make any connection between their words, their actions, and other people's experience of reality almost indiscernible. That is—it is the people who talk about God in terms of moral impositions, dogmas, and so on, who prevent discussion about God; and people who wish to enquire into reality can hardly be blamed for ignoring them.

73

There is a difference between the sort of attitude being advocated here and the old form of *laissez-faire*; not in the matter of the religious trust in the way the world works because the advocates of the old *laissez-faire* thought they trusted this, even disastrously. It is partly a recognition of the rôle man himself has to play in the free working of the world—to organise the safeguards, always personally and collectively be ready to intervene against cruelty, oppression, and so on—which the old advocates of *laissez-faire* did not do, making an ideal of what they believed in. It is this that is recognised in the west—that religious actions have to be socially responsible and political. There is no argument about this now: free action, choice, though chosen privately, is in its performance social and political: this is the form of action, the objectivity without which there is no action and no freedom. But there is some further rôle of religion here. If it is true that man's social rôle is the balancing of the respect for liberty with the demands for intervention—walking the knife-edge between the dangers of the exploitation of others on the one hand and those of one's own exploiting on the other—how is a man to achieve this balance? how to judge each instance to maintain this precariousness? The old concept of *laissez-faire* was one of the mind apart from a man's personality, conscience and honesty. Thus the decisions of people in power always seemed to work to the advantage of their passions and their greed (their own exploiting)—these being stronger when there is a split between passions and professions and nothing at the centre to hold them. The age of *laissez-faire* was an apotheosis of this—a split between what men professed to believe and what were the results of these professions—when christians said they believed in a christian world and forced small children to work fifteen hours a day in factories. To recognise the absurdity and horror of this it was necessary for people not just to theorise more about what they professed (they did this anyway) but to feel how there was something absurd and horrible about it in a personal sense—that they themselves were illogical and disgusting. But this depended on their ability to face themselves; to recognise the dangers of their passions, rationalisations and projections (the same things); and to begin to learn, to grow, to connect their theories and their behaviour, their feelings and responsibilities, in a personal and religious sense. How people might hope to do this (that it is possible and necessary to do it) is the theme of this sort of understanding. But the point here is that it is not only a person himself who is determined by this but his public and social effect. Everyone (especially a christian) cannot help having social effect; this is just his means and his results of action, his objectivity in which good or evil happens. There is little goodness, that is, except the goodness that happens to a neighbour. But whether or not this happens, and is good, will depend on what a person has made of himself: that which affects the larger issues (nowadays still often a question of corruption, ruthlessness in business) being just this sort of courage and humility.

74

Once it is admitted that the business of politics is not the single-minded pursuit of ideals but the prevention of concrete evils then a concept such as this is inescapable; the business of politics is to recognise particular evils and to face them; what it takes to do this is observation, honesty, conscience; rather than theories and idealism. And this is what the world implicitly recognises: the person who is given power is the person who is trusted: still, in spite of the enormous political cynicism of the age, it remains that people try (hope) to give responsibility and power to people who are felt to have what is called integrity—this being the characteristic of the man who faces things, does not blind himself, knows about his needs and passions and those of others, is not taken in by them. There must in some sense be needs and passions (ambition, aggression) for without them there would be no business and no politics; but what is important and is still trusted is that a person should be conscious of these and even slightly mocking—as others also necessarily will be. It is by all these processes—ambition, mockery, also tolerance of both—being held together and allowed to work freely, not only within a society but within individuals, that extremes of evil will be prevented and, as has been said, there will be growth. The means of recognising and holding these complexities both in societies and individuals should be religion—and could be, if there were not nowadays so many other things called religion. This is partly a question of ends and means. So long as it is thought that religion is to do with some ultimate and revealed ends—dogmas, moral rules, a future life, and so on—then it is natural to think that man's responsibilities are to do with these. But in the sort of understanding being advocated here it is the practical means that are man's responsibility, ends being unknowable; and the proper means are known by observing how things work. Specifically in society it is the safeguarding against evil that is man's responsibility; man knows this just by what he is, what he sees the world to be; and the end, what happens to the world, is the responsibility of God. This also seems to be the religion Christ taught. A man has to care about what he does here and now; this is his vital contact with an unknown but trusted end. But this depends on some right instinct, a right assessment from day to day; and this, in turn, on what he has done with the whole of his life—what he has learned and feels and has become from it. This is what influences the unknown end; is religious.

WHAT was once required for religious understanding was art; its job being to show something
about the world not by man's theorising or preaching
about it but by stating what was recognised in such a
way that it seemed to stand on its own, apart from a man.
Art was symbolic; people made up myths, images, and
so on, of what they loved or feared as if they would
thus be able not only to understand but to be not so
much at the mercy of it. There was the feeling that the
world was such that something vital could be said about
it in this way—there were patterns, meanings, that
could be described by symbols (what else was a symbol?)
and something that corresponded to these patterns in
man, by which he could recognise and thus deal with
them. If man tried to put his experience of meaning
into conceptual terms (his ordinary language) he came
up against paradoxes and impossibilities that seemed
due not to his own inadequacy but to that of language:
but in the symbol, the thing fashioned and discovered
on its own, these impossibilities disappeared. Art thus
became the way of saying something that could be said
in no better way; and was about the most important

things in life, what man cared about and was committed to. The business of defining things and making common-sensical statements about them was suitable for carrying on in whatever rôle had been accepted; but was no good for questions about why, or what, or what was worth-while. These questions had to be asked because without them man remained largely helpless: the world, seeming mysterious, had to be honoured and placated.

76

But when from time to time man's control over his environment increased enormously then the world ceased to seem mysterious and it was as if man's func-tion was specifically to understand it; that just by this he could control it. This was science; the idea that man's proper function was to know the world by ob-servation, experiment, the correlation of results. There was sometimes still a place for religion—which was supposed to do with what was behind the huge system of observations, what started it off and kept it going. But these were questions that were asked almost rhetoric-ally—as if they did not have much to do with life but were daydreams to satisfy some minor need in man. Also art, no longer so magical, began to be seen as that which could express what could not at the moment be expressed by science—something about people, how they worked, their actions and interactions—and thus also something of a luxury, though still not to the people producing or understanding it. But there was no open conflict between art and science and religion; science had even been a fruit of religion—christianity had taught that God had made the world and it was man's function to have power over it—and art seemed to represent something about essence, or spirit. There was some split within religion, however, which seemed as yet unobserved—to do with the fact that what man understood about religion (and had no conflict with science and art) seemed to have little to do with what he actually did about religion, this being still something magical; and also little to do with what his religion itself seemed about.

77

When man's control over his environment increased still further then a split between science and art and religion became apparent because it seemed as if man's function was just to increase the business of science infinitely—to make a complete catalogue as it were of observations and experiments and by the very totality of this to answer questions not only of how but also of why and what, or at least to render these irrelevant. People stopped asking questions about what might be at the back of the world because science seemed to have the chance of understanding everything. At the same

time in the face of scientists' claims the artists with-
drew as if their rôle was to say specifically that they
did not understand: that there was something not to
be understood in the world; that their function was to
produce patterns from the mind, the instinct; from
consciousness—forms, relations, and so on (which there
had always been in art but which now were divorced
from what they had formed, were related to)—or from
the unconscious, forces of something in an area which
science did not claim to cover because it claimed, mostly,
that it did not exist. But together with the scientists'
claim that it should in principle be possible to understand everything about everything their evidence also
began to show that it might not—that some such forces
as the artists suggested might in fact exist—even in an
area where science had tried to cover them. This was
to do with something important and uncontrollable
being recognised in the world not just in the obvious
way of recognising man's irrationality and the fact
that science even helped him in his drives towards
destruction; not just that science on its own did not
much help him towards a meaning, purpose, that still
seemed to be there; but something deeply ambiguous
within the terms of science itself. It was about this
time that in researches into the nature of the world it
began to be realised that statements that could be
made about it were not statements about facts, realities
of things, but were attempts to create models which

would explain observations: they were themselves not directly to do with whatever the things might be, but were to do with the way they worked—the things themselves remaining unknowable. Thus what had been a philosophical and religious problem (the question of what things were, and what was man to say of them) became, at the heart of things, a physical one; and this impossibility of knowing what things were in themselves was seen not as something that could be overcome by science, but as inherent in what was experienced. Some people assumed that there was now once more an area left for religion, but this was not the point (just as there being an area here for free will was not the point) because this realisation was not to do with a limitation of scientific scope as opposed to religious scope but with a limitation of the concept of knowledge. What had been realised was the fact that when man makes any statement (scientific, religious) there is no sense in his thinking that he is making a statement about the ultimate reality of a thing (whatever this might mean); but that what he is doing even about the most material things is to construct a model which will give information about his observations (experience) of what occurs. Beyond this, in the matter of what things really are, there is only the imagination: in some ways still the business of art, of religion.

78

It is here that there is a connection again between science and art and what should be religion—the sort of thing that science does having something in common with what art is trying to do; but in one sense different. Science makes its observations and constructs its models to give information in an area in which experiments can be controlled and repeated—where what is being discovered is something about sameness, probabilities, statistics. Art makes its observations and constructs its models in an area where there is no repetition and in this sense no statistics—to do with uniqueness, the single event (paradox), with man and what on its own is seen and felt and experienced. Art constructs its models which are to do with consciousness (unconsciousness) and the thing observed (known) and which are unique and paradoxical; but they are also felt to have universal significance—the unique thing, by imagination, standing for the whole. Science does not deal in totality just as it does not deal with uniqueness: it records an average: it talks of likelihood, types, rather than of significance, reality. But there is an overlapping in all these concepts: there is the recognition by science now of the interdependence of the observer and the thing observed—even that observation alters the thing observed—so that subject and object are in some sort of relation and significance: also, that there are certain phenomena only describable properly in two ways at once, a paradox. In art, there is the recognition of the force and necessity of something discursive, tentative, apart from myth and image. In both science and art there has thus been a revolution not so much about facts and ideas but in man's understanding about facts and ideas — and there might have been this kind of revolution in religion too. But in religion there seems to have been little recognition of what is happening: the same arguments go on about facts and ideas rather than about what they are and how we understand them. This is not only a pity in that religion is not doing what it should in holding together the disciplines of art and science — uniqueness and sameness — but is also absurd, because this sort of understanding has in fact always been evident (though denied) in religion. There has always been something in religion, that is, about man's proper rôle being not to talk about ultimate reality but to observe and to make models for the way things work; about the special relationship of the individual to the whole; about man's freedom thus to influence the whole; about man's perhaps having to get rid of images and talk discursively in paradoxes to do this successfully; about the fact that what does seem to alter, affect things, is in some way just the matter of observing, recognising them.

What both the Old and the New Testaments seemed to be saying was that ultimate reality (God) was unknowable but what was knowable were certain models about how to believe (worship) and how to act. It was true that through the imagining and following of these God was in a sense known; but God was not knowable in any other sense—the imagination could only feed on what was observed and practised. In the Old Testament these models were to do with laws about conduct and worship (sacrifice). Occasionally God called men mysteriously, uniquely; but this was rare, and seemed to point to the future and something new. Then in the New Testament there was this change: ultimate reality (God the Father) was still in any direct sense unknowable and what mattered was the search for, and commitment to, certain attitudes and states of mind—through which, in a sense, God was knowable. But now the necessary models were not the black-and-white rules of the Old Testament but suggestions, parables, paradoxes—unique things describable only in two ways at once—which assumed some freedom, a special relationship between the individual and the whole; matters of observing the way in which, here on earth, things worked; also implying some faith that just by recognising this, holding to it, then something of the world would be altered. All this was a subtle faith; seldom dogmatic.

What is wrong with dogmatic language is that words are taken to be descriptions of the unknowable, which prevents man's proper function. Man functions properly so long as he recognises the words (models) are to do with neither the unknowable itself nor simply his own attempted description of it but something of both, in which the connection between his understanding and reality is faith—and experience. There was a time when religious people knew this better than anyone: now other people know it and they do not. It is religious people who nowadays and for centuries argue and fight over the unknowable: seem to ignore the area in which they could reasonably argue (even conceivably fight) about experience; about what are the correct observations and models to be made from experience; what inferences can be drawn from these about what should be consciously recognised and done. Men perhaps have to try, in art, to define the indefinable: but not to fight about it. The proper area of christian argument is to do with states of mind, behaviour—what men are to do (be) about the models they have discovered (have been given) and in which they trust. A christian is in a special situation here because many of his models (religious understanding) have been given to him (are self-authenticating) in words and actions of Christ: but it is himself through experience who gives assent to these, who observes them and tries to understand them. For these models, as has been said, are paradoxical. They are things that have to be grasped, held in the mind, with effort; their meaning in practice is not clear. With such commands for instance as those about loving one's enemies, loving one's neighbour as oneself, there are questions about what is the scope of these; to whom do they refer; what has to be done on actual occasions. At different times different sorts of action may be necessary (gentleness or firmness; acceptance or refusal). Such models, for their liveliness, have to be understood, lived, not just by the mind but by the whole of a person. But it is seldom that there is a discussion of the obscurities of these. It is perhaps easier to argue in areas where there is no hope of a result rather than where might be changed oneself as well as one's neighbour.

81

What is implied by all this is, firstly, a faith in an underlying order of things—that there is an order, meaning, the effects (symptoms) of which we can observe even if we do not know what it is an order, meaning, of—and secondly, the knowledge that man's rôle in this is not just a passive one of analysing it or trying to control it as it were impersonally, but of having control over what he recognises himself as part of and committed to. This is the religious understanding that implies not only the faith that if certain attitudes are held, certain actions done, then there will be good effects (though sometimes indiscernibly); not only the demand to find out everything possible about this order (functioning) by observation and imagination and action; but also the realisation that this sort of faith, under-standing, control even, only comes alive and is effective as a result of what a man is—what he lives—not by what he does just by routine or necessity but as a result of the interaction of himself and the world in the heart. This is difficult in non-poetic language. But man does know he has this sort of freedom, perhaps his only; that this is his chance, in a world of laws, to change the world; that he is (can be) that which controls the laws (fits in with them) and these are good. It is in this understanding that he sees how the absolutes which are the concern of religion—courage, integrity, and so on— are effective not only in himself but in the world outside him. It is one of the claims of this sort of understanding that at some level people do glimpse and recognise this; that this is what life is about, not just at moments of love and fear and death but centrally, every day, from the evidence of their unique experience. Religion is a sort of scientific way of knowing uniqueness; a matter of observation and action not in the mass (impossible when observing consciousness) but in oneself in relation to other people and things. And what is found here is this connection between faith, freedom, goodness.

The way of thought that something religious has finally been revealed, something enshrined eternally in tradition, should be absurd for christian people who say they believe that this is the age of the Holy Spirit—of people being given the power to discover, act, know things for themselves. It is true there would be no Holy Spirit (as it were) if there were no God the Father (as it were) of the world's order, and no God the Son (as it were) of man's unique relationship to this. But here and now, and in the future, this is what we have been told for two thousand years but at last find ourselves landed with —man's responsibility; the bearing of it.

XI

82

MAN'S responsibility is for discovering, listening, learning; not only in science which has its own disciplines (though this is religious) but where men care mostly about life—their loves, hopes, fears, commitments. Here guides have been given—parables, actions, stories—but these are believed because of what people know and feel of them, not blindly. There are some absolutes which are to do with kindness against cruelty, courage against cowardice, faithfulness against betrayal; but even of these a purely intellectual view is equivocal (a danger of ends justifying means; a courage towards destruction) so that what has to be trusted in is a commitment with the whole of a person, an attitude learned in the whole of life. For this the religious virtues that are unambiguous are openness, receptivity, a facing and holding of things in consciousness. The vices are the closed mind, the personality untouchable, the consciousness turned in against what is feared. There is a feeling here of some ultimate value in just the extent (increasing extent) of knowledge; in man's actual growth as a result. Mystics have felt the immensity of the world; also ascetics, whose cutting-off is in order to partake of something wider. In all this there is the effort to know (experience) truth (Spirit) that both carries a man and with which he is free. The facing of his own truth gives him freedom: this is a commitment which gives him truth.

83

There remains the question of whether there is anything to be said or done about religion in the old sense —whether religion is now just something to be learned, done, by the individual in relationship to himself and those around him; or whether as in the old sense there is some specific objectivity in which relationship and truth is guaranteed. This, once, was the church and word and sacraments—the body, understanding, process, in which man could assuredly, he believed, be part of his own growth and salvation and that of the world. The phrase 'personal religion' in the old sense contained a warning —that on his own man deceived himself, that he had to have such objectivity in order not to. But now there seems the danger of man deceiving himself also by objectivity; using it to put a screen between himself and truth; and by this, the failure of his own honesty, there being also the failure of his dealings with the world. But the problem of objectivity, and truth, remains. It is thought by some that this sort of commitment to objectivity (to a body, to specific disciplines and rituals) is a necessity for man; that man is such that he will always commit himself sacramentally, that this will continue in the secular world even if not in a religious one and it is thus the job of religion to try to make its sacraments seem relevant. It is thought by others that although this has been a human need till now too often such an understanding defeats its own ends: man is called at least partly to be responsible on his own and to what he chooses. There is thus a battle at the moment between two kinds of religionists: and the only way in which one kind can be seen perhaps obviously better than the other is in that the one (those who see the dangers in objectivity, in ritual) are willing to embrace both sorts of discipline, even that which they see the dangers of: and the other (those who fear subjectivity) are not. It is this, perhaps, that is now the real revolution in Christianity. For the first time religious people are beginning to see the dangers of something (ceremony, ritual) and yet perhaps still love it; to see that there can be no truth in it perhaps in an ultimate sense unless there is some caution about what is made of it by man; to be tolerant, even, to their opponents, who are not tolerant to them. In the battle between the traditionalists and the radicals, that is, it is the traditionalists who are dangerous because they are still single minded: the radicals know that things are more paradoxical than has been supposed—ceremonies may be necessary but must be guarded against; loyalties must be loved and yet be detached from. What matters, they believe, is the truth as a person knows it; which is dependent, of course, on its being whole.

<h2 style="text-align:center">84</h2>

What is realised, then, is that the whole understanding and practice of traditional story, symbol, prayer, sacrament, and so on, either may or may not be necessary (or necessary for some and not for others) but these are questions which have no answers in the abstract; only in terms of what is experienced by those who hold to them or do not—the test of anything being, as always, its effects; what the New Testament called fruits. Everyone has to make up his own mind, that is, about what he is to do about prayer, worship, sacraments; which he does anyway, but it is just better if he admits this. The need for objectivity, discipline, is obvious; a man has to be committed (practise his commitment) in order to learn, to grow: and it is the point of prayer, worship, that this commitment at least is known; it is there for him, is able to be done. But also obvious is the need for the person to be doing something for himself; for the sake of truth. The frequent charge against the sort of attitude—trying to have it both ways—is that it produces relativism, a denial of truth; but in fact it is a trust in truth—a proclamation in the objectivity of truth itself which, if each person trusts it, can be a necessary discipline. What is experienced as relativism (weariness, cynicism) does not come from the decision to face what one truly believes and to trust this though others may believe the same thing differently; but rather from self-deception, the pretending to believe some objectivity that one does not. The real cynicism of this age is the lack of trust in truth; the violent feeling that belief has to be imposed apart from truth—even apart from what one knows as true—for fear that something might be upset, some people hurt—as if there was not an infinite hurt from just this betrayal of truth. This is the sin (fear) against the spirit of truth. At this stage of history religion does seem to be growing into some realisation of this—that truth is not held by one man against another but is possibly to be glimpsed by each in a true way: also that in each man himself truth may be something mysterious, seen in opposites. Truly religious people do seem to be those now who rather dread the religious; moral people those who are somewhat sceptical about morality. And these are not passive attitudes; they seem to be those which work, which spread religion and morality and lessen cynicism and despair. And the attitudes which do not work—do not spread religion— are those which impose rigidities and self-deceptions: which do not speak the truth for the fear of upsetting people or themselves; do not listen, enquire, for the sake of policy. All this, it seems evident, is what the New Testament is talking about: it is impossible to improve on the New Testament, only possible to talk about the same things differently. The parables and stories of the New Testament were to do with the individual faced with the immanence of heaven and hell: all men are faced with this: but now especially they are also faced with the world continuing, even of their possible under-standing and control of it through knowledge and truth (the Holy Spirit). But together with this new demand (gift) has perhaps come (is coming) a change in man's means of expression. What were once myths, images—the opposites contained within the symbol—now may have to be more discursive, conscious: no less paradoxical, but just able to state more directly (no less oddly) opposites.

85

The stories, parables, of the New Testament are in fact in this style: they are the story of the revolt against religion for the sake of religion, the getting of power by the giving up of power, the discovery of authority together with freedom: they are all there to be read, and give christians their authority and freedom. But now these stories have to be understood, acted, consciously: myth and image (unconscious) on their own are no longer lively. For the control and responsibility which is now demanded there has to be this facing of the opposites directly; a recognition and not just a yielding. This is not to say that in the matter of responsibility man will not fail: he will, always does: but he will know something of the nature of failure and in this sense (the only sense) succeed. What is (should be) happening now in the religious revolution is not something facilely optimistic —the belief that man is about to or even capable of sorting out the world—but something hopeful on a far more real level; that of understanding what the process of the world is about; knowing that failure, pain, is inherent in it, but that if truth is recognised then what happens is still of infinite goodness and worth. It is this view of man's rôle in the world—learning, listening, and then the world working for him—that has given a liveliness and confidence to religion (except that people do not call it religion) that a few years ago would have been unimaginable. This is seen in the things in which even religion in the old sense is lively—for instance in the matter of unity amongst christians. There is no longer a belief now that what men have to do in their separate conditions is argue, fight (they have not to do this just because it does not work) but rather to observe, almost be silent, in the job of trying to alter themselves (the only thing that does work) and find out about others; to act out, almost for the first time in christian history, the parable that they have always believed in—that of the mote and beam. In relations between christians and non-christians there is also something of this sudden learning and understanding; christians look, go out into the world: even the world begins to listen to christians when they talk not about their ideas (compulsions) but about experience. There is also, of course, the opposition to all this; coming from all those who think their own ideas (even if true) have to be imposed, who think that this imposition is truth even against the creation that contains it. As in Christ's day it is not only the powerfully wicked who prevent the spread of God's (man's) power in the world but also those who claim to be religious and get this wrong—even perhaps especially these, because it is they who cause the confusion in which truth is most easily hidden. Also, there is the bewilderment of those who have been faithful to their concept of religion but who still see this change as something disturbing. There has always been this predicament—the labourers in the vineyard; the sons that are not prodigal. There have to be prodigals, even bewilderment, it seems, for change.

86

Perhaps the enormous and even now remaining power and magic of religious tradition should not be played down at a time when there is too little beauty and order in the world; when men are starved of what religious ceremony can provide—the possibility of something being passionately and marvellously felt, commited to. But it is the point of all this that where there is true beauty there is subtlety and tolerance also;

there is no conflict between the true tradition and the true revolution. The church will perhaps always be the guardian of the beauty, secret; where men will go and in which they will find themselves when they look for truth, freedom, apart from themselves; what will (can) give them and the world order and meaning. This is still where there is objectivity—of speech in prayer, of action in sacrament and worship. But what there will also be is the knowledge of the danger of perverting this; that to prevent it and keep the secret true a man has to guard against the inhuman power of the form of ceremonies: has to distrust himself in his love and yielding to them. What he will trust is just the paradox, his own freedom in between the subject and object to face both ways; his own self-effacement in the faith that the world works for him, his confidence that in doing this he is free to work for the world. This sort of hope, optimism, is happening and might even be effective at a time when man's appalling capacity for evil has been experienced and recognised; it is just this that is forcing him back to responsibility; even, because of responsibility, to hope. Nowadays christians do feel there is a chance of something growing in control in the world—together with the chance of disaster. What they lack, and need, is a way to think of it—however much the traditional language once contained all this. But there has been something counterfeit about old words for so long, something exhausted about reason, a new language will have to grow, too, not be forced out of life. It will grow from this new sort of experience; the ironies, paradoxes of it; not as symbol, story, but something caught, held, nearer to meaning. It will be in art, poetry, tragedy, comedy; but art done, discussed, in terms of life, what is the meaning of life, what can be said about it: not art in terms of itself, which is meaningless. It will thus not only present itself for people to do as they like with but have its own authority, communicativeness and even reason: perhaps even its attempts to define the indefinable; its definitions experience.

87

The feeling of the present age is that there is something racing against time; man's control rushing with his forces to destroy himself, these two equal and inescapable. It is absurd to think man may not destroy himself; equally to think there is anything unusual to fear. All through history man has been haunted by this will to chaos and destruction; now he knows what haunts him, which is his hope and chance of defeating it. For thousands of years he has tried to prove himself by aggression, blame, self-justification; this has arisen from his own weakness and incapacity and this he has projected on to the world; now he knows, and can alter it in himself. But at the same time he has the power to destroy himself. There has always been this choice in a symbolic, individual form: now it is real and total. Yet all that can be altered, still, is himself; who in turn can alter the world. In this extraordinary situation man can now do what he has always hoped for but which now having the power seems almost beyond him; what he dreamed of in the dark is now in the light. There are some signs of his choosing; a slight spreading of peace, a few corners of responsibility. There is also breakdown, neurosis, the teeming millions. This is a time when all battles are becoming moral again: suddenly categories are clearer (now morals are obsolete); on the one hand the people of observable obstinacy and breakdown, on the other those who listen and are human. These have nothing to do with old moral categories; they are categories of what is odd and truthful against what is plain and self-deceptive. There is the choice between these in oneself and in the world. There is a commitment either with courage or with the lack of it; a carrying-on in faith or a refusal of it. Courage causes and is the result of faith: self-deception causes and is the result of lack of courage. There is a circle, not vicious, in which choice is still possible. It is no longer useful to ask how the choice is made: it happens, at the attempt at it.

88

For christians this is a special time (as always) because if it is true that man now has to be on his own in order to take responsibility then christians are people uniquely fitted for this because they are not; they have some experience, however inexpressible, of what works with and for them. This is an experience of human faith, freedom; only christian in the special sense of naming it. And if christians know about this experience of the Holy Spirit they also know about the mixture of tragedy and comedy: they know that man may fail but that there is no reason not to have faith in man, that the world may end but there is no reason not to achieve the success of the world. They know all this because of what they learn here and now: this is what the world is like, beauty and pain, the insufferability and wonder of it. This is a time for christians to be strictly practical and truthful; to behave (and speak and write) according to what they know, experience—in faith in creation and even by this to recognise transcendence. But in doing this (and finding it) they should not believe it will be obvious: all behaviour (speech, writing) contains its own oddities; what succeeds is only what occurs. Christians and others do know all this: with the enormous increase in knowledge and power and danger there is again humility and awe (the beginning); also a rush of life, energy. The world has meaning, is tragic: man can alter it (redeem). This is the point (it is done for him) in religion.

About the Author

Born in London on June 25, 1923, Nicholas Mosley was educated at Eton and Oxford. He served in Italy during World War II, and published his first novel, *Spaces of the Dark*, in 1951. Since then, he has published sixteen works of fiction, including the novels *Accident, Impossible Object*, and *Hopeful Monsters*, winner of the 1990 Whitbread Award. Mosley is also the author of several works of nonfiction, most notably the autobiography *Efforts at Truth* and a biography of his father, Sir Oswald Mosley, *Rules of the Game/Beyond the Pale*. He currently resides in London.

SELECTED DALKEY ARCHIVE PAPERBACKS

FOR A FULL LIST OF PUBLICATIONS, VISIT:
w w w . d a l k e y a r c h i v e . c o m

SELECTED DALKEY ARCHIVE PAPERBACKS

FOR A FULL LIST OF PUBLICATIONS, VISIT:
www.dalkeyarchive.com